"HARNESSING AI: TRANSFORMING COMMERCE AND MANAGEMENT"

DR. SHRADDHA SENGAR AND
DR. ANUBHUTI SHARMA

Contents

Contents

Preface

""Artificial Intelligence is not just about machines thinking; it's about humans thinking better with machines.""

The world is witnessing an unprecedented revolution driven by Artificial Intelligence (AI), reshaping industries, redefining commerce, and transforming management practices. Harnessing AI: Transforming Commerce and Management explores this dynamic landscape, offering insights into the profound ways AI is influencing the way we conduct business and manage organizations.

This book is designed for professionals, academics, and students eager to understand AI's potential and applications in commerce and management. It delves into how AI-powered tools and technologies are enhancing decision-making, streamlining operations, and enabling personalized customer experiences. From predictive analytics and robotic process automation to smart supply chains and AI-driven leadership strategies, this book covers a spectrum of topics crucial for thriving in an AI-driven economy.

The chapters aim to provide a balanced perspective—examining both the opportunities and challenges that come with integrating AI into commercial and managerial practices. Ethical considerations, workforce transformation, and the need for upskilling are addressed, ensuring a holistic understanding of the implications of AI adoption.

As you journey through these pages, you will discover how AI can empower businesses to innovate, adapt, and stay competitive in an ever-evolving global marketplace. By embracing the ideas and strategies discussed, readers will be better equipped to harness the transformative power of AI and lead the change in their respective fields.

I hope this book serves as a guide, an inspiration, and a call to action for everyone striving to make a meaningful impact in the era of AI.

Happy reading!!

Dr. Shradhha Sengar

Dr. Anubhuti Sharma

Acknowledgements

With the grace of the Almighty, we extend our deepest gratitude to everyone who made this publication possible. The papers compiled in this volume represent the collaborative efforts of academicians, industry professionals, and students, whose valuable contributions we gratefully acknowledge. We remain intellectually indebted to them.

We are profoundly thankful to Dr. Shikha Agrawal and Dr. Sr. Alice Thomas for their unwavering guidance and enlightenment, as well as to our academic team for their insightful suggestions and steadfast encouragement.

Our heartfelt appreciation goes to our family, friends, and colleagues for their unwavering support and belief in us throughout this journey.

Special Thanks to our Ph.D. Guides Prof. (Dr.) Manisha Pandey. Her guidance, wisdom and encouragement have shaped our academic and professional journey.

A special note of thanks to the publishing team for their professionalism and dedication. To all who have supported this endeavour, directly or indirectly, we are deeply grateful for your integral role in this accomplishment.

With sincere appreciation,

Top of Form

Dr. Shradhha Sengar

Dr. Anubhuti Sharma

Disclaimer

The Authors are solely responsible for the contents published in the book. The publisher and editor do not take any responsibility for the same in any manner. Error, if any, is purely unintentional and readers are requested to communicate such error to the editors or publisher to avoid discrepancies in future.

All Right Reserved

The characters and events portrayed in this book are fictitious. Any similarity to real persons, living or dead is coincidental and not intended by the authors.

No part of this book may be reproduced, or stored in a retrieval system, or transmitted in any form or by any means, electronic, mechanical, photocopying, recording, or otherwise, without express written permission of the publisher.

ISBN: 979-88-9475-905-0

Price: Rs.

Published & Printed by: Notion Press Publishing

(www.notionpress.com)

About Editors

Dr. Shraddha Sengar is an accomplished academic and industry professional with over 12 years of extensive experience. Currently serving as an Assistant Professor at the Graduate School of Business, Indore, she plays a pivotal role in advancing the institution's Public Relations and Vibrancy initiatives. She holds a Ph.D. in Management from Renaissance University, Indore, and an MBA from Devi Ahilya Vishwavidyalaya, Indore, with a research focus on Human Resource Management and Marketing.

Dr. Sengar is a certified SAP ERP professional and an accredited POSH (Prevention of Sexual Harassment) trainer, reflecting her commitment to fostering ethical and technology-driven practices in management. Her academic contributions are significant, with numerous research papers published in prestigious outlets, including Scopus-indexed, ABDC-listed, UGC CARE-approved, and other peer-reviewed journals. These works emphasize innovative strategies in HR and Marketing, often integrating sustainable development themes.

As an invited speaker at national and international platforms, Dr. Sengar is recognized for her expertise in aligning Human Resource strategies with the United Nations' Sustainable Development Goals (SDGs). Her thought leadership and multidisciplinary approach continue to inspire students, academics, and professionals alike, making her a key contributor to the field of management education.

About Editors

Dr. Anubhuti Sharma is a highly experienced academician and researcher with an impressive career spanning over 19 years, including 15 years in academia and 4 years in the corporate sector. She holds a Ph.D. and an MBA from IMS, Devi Ahilya Vishwavidyalaya, Indore, and has further expanded her expertise with a certification in Business Analytics from IIM Kozhikode. She is an Associate Professor and currently, serving as the Head of the Department of Management at St. Paul Institute of Professional Studies, where she is responsible for driving academic initiatives and fostering a culture of excellence in management education. She also serves as the IIC President, Head of the Research Cell, and NAAC Coordinator of the institute.

Dr. Sharma is deeply committed to research and professional development. She has authored more than 35 research papers published in leading journals, including Scopus-indexed, ABDC-listed, and UGC CARE-approved publications. Her scholarly work reflects a strong focus on contemporary issues in management and innovative approaches to business challenges. Dr. Sharma is also an active participant in international and national conferences, Faculty Development Programs (FDPs), and seminars, continually contributing to and learning from the broader academic and professional community.

Her dual experience in academia and the industry allows her to offer a balanced perspective on management education, blending theoretical frameworks with practical insights. With her dynamic leadership, Dr. Sharma inspires both students and colleagues, ensuring the department stays at the forefront of management education and research.

CHAPTER I

"Artificial Intelligence the game changer in HR"

Prof. (Dr.) Shikha Agrawal
(Principal, Graduate School of Business, Indore)

Abstract

Industry 5.0 talks all about use of Information Technology and Artificial Intelligence in the business world. As an outcome of this today's HR professionals strive to optimize the mix of human and automated processes for a simple, seamless and intuitive workplace. It gives them the opportunity to be creative, intelligent and able to provide a competitive and effective workforce. While HR seems to support the use of AI in relation to operations or other business organizations such as marketing and sales, HR can influence AI management. In people management studies, the influence of intelligence on intelligence has expanded further. It goes from the employee onboarding to exit process, including training, onboarding, benefits, information, and more. Here are some key issues. This article describes the current AI focused HR work and focuses on its future. This paper explains about the present HR functions that are AI driven and also focuses on the future of it.

Keywords: Artificial Intelligence, future, Human Resource

Introduction

Artificial intelligence (AI) has changed many industries so quickly that Sophia, an advanced AI robot, participated in a panel and competition during the United Nations Conference on Sustainable

Development. AI offers a variety of solutions for hiring managers, including recruiting tools, middleware applications, and advanced AI solutions. Together or independently, these tools create a better way for HR to predict a candidate's future success at the company. Artificial Intelligence is revolutionizing HR in the context of Industry 5.0.

Artificial Intelligence is a technology that allows machines to think, know and complete the work that humans have done before. As a dominant component of Industry 5.0 artificial intelligence has grown exponentially over the past decade. Artificial intelligence helps IT companies make better and faster decisions. This applies not only to the HR field, but also to other fields. Human resources professionals use artificial intelligence software to drive faster onboarding and create greater efficiency throughout the hiring and selection process. AI technology holds great promise for advancing the HR profession.

In computer science, artificial intelligence (AI), sometimes called machine intelligence, is intelligence displayed by machines as opposed to intelligence displayed by humans and other animals. Computer science defines the work of intelligence as the work of "intelligent people": any device that knows its surroundings and works to achieve its goals. Kaplan and Hahnlein define intelligence as "the ability of a system to accurately interpret external information, learn from this information, and use that learning to achieve goals and objectives through flexible adaptation". Colloquially, the term "intelligence" is used when a machine (such as "learning" and "problem solving") mimics the "knowledge" of human activity in relation to other human minds. Industry 5.0 talks about making the most of artificial intelligence.

Artificial intelligence is one of the most important tools for the advancement of the entire industry and a major component of Industry 5.0, and the same is true for human resources. Although

HR are a group of people managing people, AI will continue to play a big role in changing the HR process by making it more transparent, efficient and successful. At a broader level, HR will be able to analyses simple trends, find and compare patterns, and use this information to make decisions with techniques such as machine learning. AI will help HR gather more important information about the people who will change the HR function. All HR professionals talk about identity. It may seem strange, but AI can help improve people in the business world.

There is no doubt that the impact of artificial intelligence on HR will be clear and sustainable over time. Technology is constantly changing, which means your AI framework has to evolve to adapt and change as needed. AI will be used to eliminate most HR tasks, analyze large volumes of data for decision making, and make an impact on your organization and its employees.

Literature Review

M. Sriram, L. Gandhi, D.Manjunatheshwara(2017) in their research work iterated that artificial intelligence and machine learning in the HR function of the IT industry - try to build a research-based model Results This article covers machine learning. Some selected case studies of companies were used to demonstrate how they will transform their HR processes using. As a result, there are many new ways machine learning and AI can be used in HR functionality.

Ian Bailie(2018) commented thatAI is designed for people who want to learn more about the potential use of skills in human resources. They studied business and education to create representatives of artificial intelligence and its applications in business, with a particular focus on human resources. The report also used key research, research findings, and interviews with vendors and experts from the Cognition X AI-powered HR product catalog. It focused on various issues related to the cost of implementing new AI tools, technology from a ROI perspective, human resources and skills to work with AI, and honest decision-making when using AI technology.

Vivek Yawalkar (2019) this research article explained the situation that among the many tasks performed, artificial intelligence has many human services. Some AI based services are done by robots. Companies can perform recruitment, hiring, data analysis, data collection, reducing office work and making a good impact on the employees and clients both.

Cliff Saran (2019) IT decision makers are increasingly aware of artificial intelligence (AI) bias, according to a survey of 350 US and UK CIOs, CFOs, VPs and IT executives. Almost half of AI experts in the US and UK say they are "very" to "rarely" concerned about AI bias. A survey by Data Robot revealed that organizations are using AI to work across departments, including HR (35%). The survey also revealed that 85 percent of IT executives surveyed believe that AI management will help improve operations.

Geeta R & B.S Reddy D (2021), examined how artificial intelligence affects recruitment strategies. The research also shed light on the artificial intelligence that companies use when recruiting. The research was based on secondary data such as practical documents, various journal reviews, books, and websites used for further research. Other sources such as websites, journals, publications, publications and books were referenced in full text. Ultimately, this is what AI does – it is the integration of humans and AI that leads to data management, saving organizations costs and time, and providing greater accuracy and access throughout the hiring process.

Research Methodology

The study is based on secondary method of data composed from research papers, printed resources, online websites, HR blogs, and survey reports available by various IT companies and research organisations. The paper uses more of secondary and current data from various platforms to discuss the present situation of HR in companies in the use of Artificial Intelligence.

Discussions

In the present era the various HR functions that are AI driven are as follows:

- **Employee attrition research:** Identify employees at risk of leaving; this eliminates the guesswork that normally is done at the HR level. Once such employees are identified the HR can engage them in discussions, and retain them.
- **Personal Information Flow:** Provide users with personal information by recommending business and education services through predictive analytics.
- **Finding Bad Data:** Identify events and observations that do not fit certain patterns in the data and remove them from source and also make sure they are not a part of the system again.
- **Speech Recognition:** While many aspects of human speech and voice are difficult to understand, deep learning can recognize and respond to human speech, making it possible to solve problems.
- **Chatbots:** NLP (Natural Language Processing) trains chat bots to understand human language, voice and context and has become a significant potential for automating HR services.
- **Digital assistants:** Digital assistants are interactive platforms where users can ask questions in their own words. For example, digital assistants can assist new employees with tasks and advise on what to do next, helping employees get the answers they need

quickly without having to navigate through many documents or web pages and waste time working.

- **Identifying Best Candidates**: Find the best person for the job based on skills and experience. In addition to simply searching for keywords, machine learning algorithms learn the most common keywords used in the text. Candidates found through organic or targeted search are encouraged to apply for open positions. AI can alert people with the right skills to job postings before they are posted.

- **Forecasting Candidate Performance**: Artificial intelligence-based candidate that matches HR data to determine the candidate's likelihood of accepting the job, performance results, and forecast job. Using digital assistants to provide applicants with more information is a key advantage of AI at the interview stage; share notes and approve reviews.

- **Pick and Place**: Machine learning should not be used to make final decisions, but AI can help recruiters and managers make better hiring decisions. Use references and professional acumen to match job opportunities with top talent in similar roles at your company.

- **Create Job Opportunities**: Check out lots of information about local businesses and competitive salaries that provide detailed information on how jobs should be filled. In particular, AI can increase recruitment efficiency by calculating a candidate's probability of accepting a job based on the candidate's personal and work history.

- **Reduce administrative burden**: Send and receive important documents, company policies and login credentials. AI can track which documents have been viewed, collect electronic signatures when each step is completed, eliminating the need for manual tracking by HR.

- **Reduce production time**: AI-powered digital assistants suggest learning about the job and provide relevant information, such as books and magazines, based on how well employees perform in similar tasks.

- **Create Market Analysis:** AI analyzes a wide range of salary data and available competitive data about the local market to provide a better picture and strategy of how the business should be segmented.
- **Improve Employment:** Improve recruiting by comparing job characteristics with an employee and employee history to determine the likelihood of hiring a candidate.
- **Improve the employee experience:** With a high level of automation and a focus on the customer experience in the environment, employees want to be efficient and effective even when engaged in personal engagement. Today, technology-based consumers shape employee experiences and seek options for what they want to interact with and support. Periodic information can be used by businesses, but many organizations still rely on manual processes to draw insights and decisions from the information. This job often involves data analysts and therefore causes delays in visualization. Decisions still use outdated or outdated information.
- **Automation and Intelligence:** Intelligent automation is a combination of intelligence and automation that allows machines to understand, understand, learn and act on their own or with little help. Intelligent automation not only does manual work, it also makes sense and decisions like humans. Its ability enables machines to understand processes and their differences. Not only that, AI can also be incorporated into all iterations to increase efficiency, productivity and drive innovation.

Artificial intelligence in Human Capital Management: AI plays a key role in bringing together key HR functions to transform the entire employee experience ecosystem. It focuses on creating technical systems to reduce employee turnover and manage important functions such as business management, business planning, people analysis, career paths and personal service.

According to a study by Deloitte Bersin, approximately 40 percent of companies use some form of intelligence in their HR functions. The HR applications of artificial intelligence are by far the most important in the recruitment process.

They improve and refine the recruitment process, remove bias and gender language from the job record, evaluate applicants' responses to screening questions, schedule follow-up interviews, screen for candidate valuations, and even send attentive automated emails to candidates after recruitment for the interview.

Organizations are increasingly using solutions that combine machine learning, natural language processing and sentiment analysis for more complex applications. In the process, they are changing the HR function while freeing and empowering HR staff to focus on different initiatives. For example, the deep analytical capabilities of AI enable managers to intelligently understand the risk and financial impact of attrition, enabling them to take mitigation measures. Meanwhile, data visualization tools like heat maps and word clouds measure trends in discrimination and injustice, politics and hierarchy, and other issues in workforce participation and diversity.

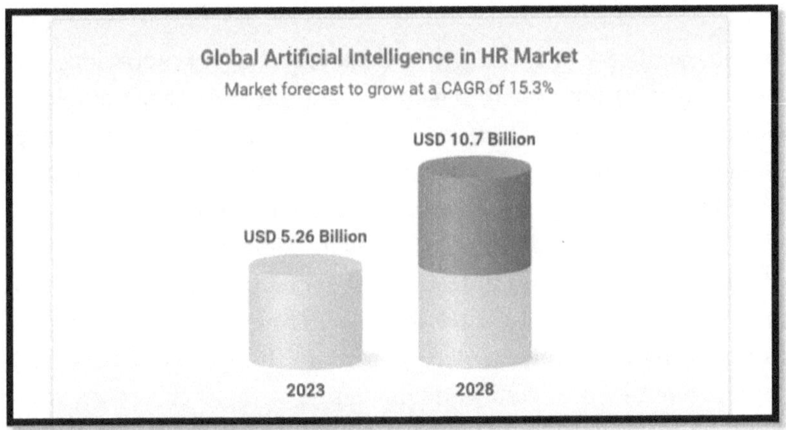

Source: https://www.researchandmarkets.com/reports/ 5567002/global-artificial-intelligence-in-hr-market

According to the report presented by researchandmarkets.com the market of Artificial Intelligence in HR from the year 2023 to 2028 will grow at a rate of 15.3% and in 2028 shall be valued at $10.7 Billion. The AI in HR market is found to be valued at $5.26 Billion in 2023. The growth rate is high and phenomenal. This shows that in the coming years Industry 5.0 shall thrust on AI in the Human Resource domain. It is forecasted that AI will drive most innovation in nearly every field in the next 1-5 years. Some even believe that artificial intelligence and machine learning will help HR managers reduce their work while improving overall business performance.

Conclusion

Indeed, artificial intelligence has provided a very efficient and precise system for human business solutions. AI makes employee retention, talent management, employee development, employee evaluation, employee compensation, employee selection, coordination among employees, tracking employee performance and collaboration, and other tasks easier. HR managers must decide which technology to use in HR. While some researchers say that AI cannot replace the critical feedback of HR, others believe that AI will soon replace the critical function of HR as it has a better HR approach in terms of errors and quick response. At this stage, when AI and HR are integrated, the HR manager will decide how much AI should be used in the HR function.

A clear distinction should be made between tasks managed by AI and those of HR management, and AI should be complemented by HR impact on all functions. HR is responsible for knowledge of important social behaviors and minds of people. Companies cannot retain their employees or their trust in the company if all responsibilities are delegated to robots. AI can be a tool, not a master.

Reference & Bibliography

1. https://papers.ssrn.com/sol3/papers.cfm?abstract_id=326387
2. https://papers.ssrn.com/sol3/papers.cfm?abstract_id=3263878
3. http://hj.diva-portal.org/smash/get/diva2:1322478/FULLTEXT01.pdf
4. https://www.ey.com/Publication/vwLUAssets/EY-the-new-age-artificial-intelligence-for-human-resource-opportunities-and-functions/$FILE/EY-the-new-age-artificial-intelligence-for-human-resource-opportunities-and-functions.pdf
5. https://www.employmentstudies.co.uk/system/files/resources/files/

mp142_The_impact_of_Artificial_Intelligence_on_the_HR_function-Peter_Reilly.pdf

6.https://www.employmentstudies.co.uk/system/files/resources/files/

mp142_The_impact_of_Artificial_7.Intelligence_on_the_HR_function Peter_Reilly.pdf   8.https://www.sciencedirect.com/science/article/pii/S0149206396900136

9.https://knowledge.wharton.upenn.edu/article/using-ai-in-human-resources/   10.https://www.cmswire.com/digital-workplace/7-ways-artificial-intelligence-is-reinventing-human-resources/

11.https://www.aragoconsulting.eu/en/tips-best-practices/6-biggest-challenges-hr-function-2019-artificial-intelligence-process-automation-hr-chatbot

12.https://www.computerweekly.com/news/252474408/IT-chiefs-recognise-the-risks-of-artificial-intelligence-bias.

CHAPTER II

"Balancing Innovation and Responsibility: Ethical Issues in Autonomous AI Decision-Making"

Dr. Anubhuti Sharma
Associate Professor, St. Paul Institute of Professional Studies, Indore
Mr. Aaradhya Sharma
Pursuing B. Tech. in Aero Space, VIT, Bhopal

Abstract

This research paper delves into the ethical implications of autonomous decision-making within artificial intelligence (AI) systems. As AI technology advances, it is crucial to address concerns related to transparency, fairness, and accountability in AI algorithms. The study examines how ethical frameworks can be integrated into the design and implementation of AI to ensure responsible and unbiased decision-making. Additionally, it explores the societal impact of autonomous AI, focusing on issues such as privacy, job displacement, and inherent biases. The aim is to provide insights into developing ethical guidelines that foster innovation while mitigating the unintended consequences of AI technology.

Keywords: AI ethics, Autonomous decision-making, Transparency, Accountability, Bias, Privacy

Introduction

Artificial Intelligence (AI) has become a transformative force, significantly impacting various sectors, from healthcare to finance and beyond. As AI technologies evolve, one of the critical challenges for researchers, developers, and policymakers is navigating the ethical dimensions of autonomous decision-making. Autonomous AI decision-making refers to the ability of AI systems to independently make choices and draw conclusions without direct human intervention. "Autonomous" implies that the AI system can operate and make decisions based on its programming, training, and the data it has encountered.

Key characteristics of autonomous AI decision-making include:

Independence: The AI system functions without continuous human oversight, making decisions in real-time based on available data.

Learning Capability: These systems often employ machine learning algorithms, enabling them to learn from data and refine their decision-making processes over time.

Complex Decision Spaces: They can handle vast decision spaces with numerous possible actions or outcomes, which is vital for applications like self-driving cars, medical diagnostics, and financial analysis.

Real-time Decision-Making: Autonomous AI can make rapid decisions, essential in scenarios that require quick responses, such as automated manufacturing or autonomous vehicles.

Examples of applications include:

Autonomous Vehicles: Self-driving cars make real-time decisions about navigation, traffic, and safety.

Healthcare Diagnostics: AI systems autonomously analyze medical images to assist in diagnosing diseases.

Financial Trading: AI algorithms autonomously decide on buying or selling financial instruments based on market data.

Industrial Automation: AI-driven systems autonomously manage and optimize manufacturing processes, adapting to changing conditions and minimizing downtime.

While the benefits of autonomous AI decision-making are numerous, they also raise ethical concerns, such as potential biases, transparency issues, and accountability challenges. Addressing these concerns is essential to balance the innovation offered by AI with ethical and responsible deployment.

Literature Review

The rapid development of AI brings forth innovative applications but also raises significant ethical concerns, particularly in the realm of autonomous decision-making. This literature review synthesizes key insights from existing research, examining the ethical considerations of balancing innovation and accountability in AI systems.

Diakopoulos (2016) discusses the concept of "Algorithmic Accountability," highlighting the challenges of holding AI accountable for its decisions. The study emphasizes the importance of transparency in the decision-making process and the underlying algorithms, advocating for practices that allow for external scrutiny. This aligns with the increasing demand for 'algorithmic transparency' as a fundamental aspect of ethical AI.

Recent advances in explainable AI (XAI) (Guidotti et al., 2018) provide a promising solution to these ethical challenges. Explainability enhances the interpretability of AI decisions, serving as a bridge between complex algorithms and human understanding. As the ethical implications of autonomous AI decision-making are explored, it is essential to consider the role of XAI in achieving a balance between innovation and accountability.

In conclusion, this literature review presents diverse viewpoints, highlighting the need for a nuanced understanding of the ethical considerations in autonomous AI decision-making. From value alignment and algorithmic transparency to ethics by design and Explainability, this review sets the stage for further exploration of the interplay between innovation and accountability in AI ethics.

Objectives

1.To investigate and analyze the ethical accountability of autonomous AI decision-making.

2.To develop recommendations and strategies for balancing the innovative potential of autonomous AI with the need for accountability and ethical considerations.

Research Methodology

Type of Research : Descriptive
Population : All respondents
Data (Sample Size) : 75 respondents
Type of Sampling : Convenient Random Sampling
Data collection Methods : Survey Method
Data Collection Tool : Structured Questionnaire
Data Analysis Tool : Chi square test of association

Primary data was used to conduct the research, collected through structured questionnaires completed by respondents. These questionnaires were designed after a thorough literature review to analyze the ethical considerations in autonomous AI decision-making, specifically focusing on balancing innovation and accountability.

Analysis and Interpretation

Hypothesis for Objective 1:

- **H01**: There is no statistically significant association between the belief that autonomous AI systems can foster positive innovation in decision-making processes and the accountability attributed to organizations using autonomous AI.
- **H11**: There is a statistically significant association between the belief that autonomous AI systems can foster positive innovation in decision-making processes and the accountability attributed to organizations using autonomous AI.

Hypothesis for Objective 2:

- **H02**: There is no need for specific recommendations and strategies to balance the innovative potential of autonomous AI decision-making with accountability and ethical considerations
- **H12**: Specific recommendations and strategies are needed to balance the innovative potential of autonomous AI decision-making with accountability and ethical considerations.

Analysis

The test of association assumes that the variables are independent in the null hypothesis. If the test reveals a significant association, it indicates that the variables are not independent, thus providing evidence against the null hypothesis.

- **H01**: There is no statistically significant association between the belief that autonomous AI systems can foster positive innovation in decision-making processes and the accountability attributed to organizations using autonomous AI.

- **H11**: There is statistically significant association between the belief that autonomous AI systems can foster positive innovation in decision-making processes and the accountability attributed to organizations using autonomous AI.

Contingency Tables 1					
		organizations using autonomous AI should be responsible for the unethical decisions			
Belief that autonomous AI systems can bring positive innovation to decision-making processes		Very Responsible	Responsible	not Responsible	Total
Disagree		0	14	0	14
Neutral		3	9	6	18
Agree		10	28	0	38
Strongly Agree		0	5	0	5
Total		13	56	6	75

Contingency Tables 1					
		organizations using autonomous AI should be responsible for the unethical decisions			
Belief that autonomous AI systems can bring positive innovation to decision-making processes		Very Responsible	Responsible	not Responsible	Total

χ^2 Tests			
	Value	df	p
χ^2	27.2	6	< .001
N	75		

Chi-Square Test:

The chi-square statistic is 27.2 with 6 degrees of freedom, indicating a significant association between the belief in positive innovation and views on organizational responsibility for unethical decisions. The p-value (< .001) is below the conventional significance level of 0.05, providing strong evidence to reject the null hypothesis.

Summary:

The results demonstrate a statistically significant relationship between individuals' beliefs in the positive innovation potential of autonomous AI systems and their opinions on organizational responsibility for unethical decisions. This finding suggests that changes in individuals' beliefs about positive innovation are associated with corresponding changes in their views on organizational responsibility for unethical decisions.

In summary, the data supports the idea that individuals' attitudes towards the positive innovation potential of autonomous AI systems are linked to their expectations of organizational accountability for unethical AI-related decisions.

Hypotheses:

- H02: There is no need for specific recommendations and strategies to balance the innovative potential of autonomous AI decision-making with accountability and ethical considerations.
- **H02 (a):** There is no significant correlation between respondents' concerns about potential biases in autonomous AI decision-making and the need to address and mitigate these biases to ensure fairness.
- **H12 (a):** There is a significant correlation between respondents' concerns about potential biases in autonomous AI decision-

making and the need to address and mitigate these biases to ensure fairness.

Contingency Tables 2

Ensure Fairness	Potential Biasness in AI Decisions			Total
	concerned	Neutral	Not Concerned	
Very Important	9	0	0	9
Important	35	8	0	43
neutral	5	12	0	17
not important	3	0	3	6
Total	52	20	3	75

χ^2 Tests

	Value	df	p
χ^2	58.2	6	< .001
N	75		

Chi-Square Test:

The chi-square statistic is 58.2 with 6 degrees of freedom, indicating a highly significant association between individuals' perceptions of potential bias in AI decision-making and their levels of concern. The p-value (< .001) is below the conventional significance level of 0.05, providing strong evidence to reject the null hypothesis.

Summary:

The results indicate a statistically significant relationship between individuals' views on the importance of ensuring fairness in AI decisions and their levels of concern regarding potential bias. This suggests that as individuals place greater importance on fairness in AI decisions, their concern about potential bias tends to increase.

In conclusion, the data demonstrates a significant association between individuals' attitudes towards ensuring fairness in AI decisions and their concerns about potential bias, highlighting the need to address these issues.

Hypotheses:

- **H02(b):** There is no significant correlation between individuals being informed about the use of autonomous AI in decision-making that directly affects them and their concerns about potential privacy invasion due to AI deployment.
- **H12(b):** There is a significant correlation between individuals being informed about the use of autonomous AI in decision-making that directly affects them and their concerns about potential privacy invasion due to AI deployment.

Contingency Tables 3

| | Invasion of privacy | | | |
Informed use of AI	Very Concerned	concerned	Neutral	Total
Completely informed	21	9	0	30
informed	0	14	0	14
neutral	8	4	8	20
not important	5	2	4	11
Total	34	29	12	75

χ^2 Tests

	Value	df	p
χ^2	44.8	6	< .001
N	75		

Recommendations

1. Develop comprehensive ethical guidelines for autonomous AI decision-making that emphasize fairness, transparency, and accountability.

2. Establish clear ethical standards to guide developers, organizations, and policymakers in the responsible deployment of AI systems.

3. Emphasize transparency in AI algorithms and decision-making processes to improve their explainability.

4. Implement mechanisms that offer clear and understandable explanations for AI decisions, building user trust and ensuring accountability.

5. Integrate ethics training into the education and professional development of AI developers.

6.Ensure developers are knowledgeable about ethical considerations, promoting a proactive approach to addressing ethical issues during the design and development stages.

7.Empower users by giving them control over their data and the decisions made by autonomous AI systems.

8.Design user-friendly interfaces that allow individuals to understand, influence, and challenge decisions made by AI algorithms that affect them.

9.Conduct regular, independent ethical audits of autonomous AI systems to evaluate their compliance with ethical guidelines.

10.Create a framework for ongoing monitoring and evaluation, addressing ethical concerns as technology advances.

These recommendations are intended to help stakeholders navigate the ethical challenges of autonomous AI decision-making, balancing innovation with accountability, and fostering a responsible and ethical AI ecosystem.

Conclusion

In the fast-paced realm of autonomous AI decision-making, addressing ethical considerations is essential to balance innovation with accountability. The recommendations provided underscore the necessity of a comprehensive and forward-looking approach to tackle the ethical challenges associated with AI systems. Establishing clear ethical guidelines is crucial, providing a foundation for developers, organizations, and policymakers to incorporate ethical principles throughout the AI development process. Transparency and explainability are key, enhancing user trust and accountability by clarifying AI decision-making processes.

References

1. Henriksen, S. Enni, and A. Bechmann (2021), "Situated accountability: Ethical principles, certification standards, and explanation methods in applied AI," in Proceedings of the 2021 AAAI/ACM Conference on AI, Ethics, and Society, pp. 574–585.
2. Jobson, V. Mar, and I. Freckelton (2022), "Legal and ethical considerations of artificial intelligence in skin cancer diagnosis," Australasian Journal of Dermatology, vol. 63, no. 1, pp. e1–e5.
3. Belenguer (2022), "AI bias: exploring discriminatory algorithmic decision-making models and the application of possible machine-centric solutions adapted from the pharmaceutical industry," AI and Ethics, vol. 2, no. 4, pp. 771–787.
4. Katell et al. (2020), "Toward situated interventions for algorithmic equity: lessons from the field," in Proceedings of the 2020 conference on fairness, accountability, and transparency, pp. 45–55.
5. Mehrabi, F. Morstatter, N. Saxena, K. Lerman, and A. Galstyan (2021), "A survey on bias and fairness in machine learning," ACM computing surveys (CSUR), vol. 54, no. 6, pp. 1–35.
6. William, N. Yogeesh, S. Vimala, and P. Gite (2022), "Blockchain Technology for Data Privacy using Contract Mechanism for 5G Networks," 3rd International Conference on Intelligent Engineering and Management (ICIEM), IEEE, 2022, pp. 461–465.
7. Gorur, L. Hoon, and E. Kowal (2020), "Computer Science Ethics Education in Australia–A Work in Progress," IEEE International Conference on Teaching, Assessment, and Learning for Engineering (TALE), IEEE, pp. 945–947.
8. B. Jaman, A. H. Nuraeni, B. P. Pitaloka, and K. Z. Gadri (2022), "Juridical Analysis Simplification of Environmental Permits Integrated Through Business Permits Regulated in Law Number 11 of 2020 Concerning Job Creation," Libertas Law Journal, vol. 1, no. 1, pp. 10–22.
9. Bogina, A. Hartman, T. Kuflik, and A. Shulner Tal (2021), "Educating software and AI stakeholders about algorithmic

fairness, accountability, transparency and ethics," International Journal of Artificial Intelligence in Education, pp. 1–26.

10. Tolmeijer, M. Christen, S. Kandul, M. Kneer, and A. Bernstein (2022), "Capable but amoral? Comparing AI and human expert collaboration in ethical decision making," in Proceedings of the 2022 CHI Conference on Human Factors in Computing Systems, pp. 1–17.

CHAPTER III

"Effectiveness of AI–Driven Training Modules with a Focus on Demographic Variables"

Dr. Shraddha Sengar
(Assistant Professor, Graduate School of Business, Indore)

Abstract

This research focuses on the effectiveness of AI-driven training modules, with a specific emphasis on how demographic factors such as age, qualification, and gender impact key aspects of employee development. The study delves into several dimensions, including engagement, learning retention, user satisfaction, skill development, and cost-effectiveness, to understand how these elements differ across diverse demographic groups. Using a combination of extensive literature review and primary data gathered through structured questionnaires, the research evaluates how AI-powered modules influence learning outcomes for employees with varying demographic profiles. The study explores how AI-driven training can be personalized to meet the needs of different age groups, educational backgrounds, and genders, providing insights into how these factors shape the overall effectiveness of training programs. The findings aim to offer valuable guidance to HR professionals and organizational leaders, enabling them to optimize their training strategies by integrating AI technologies in a way that caters to the unique needs of their diverse workforce. Ultimately, the research aims to contribute to the ongoing conversation about the future of training and development in the digital era, emphasizing the importance of demographic considerations in shaping effective training approaches.

Introduction

Training and development are integral components of Human Resources (HR) that significantly influence an organization's success. Effective training programs not only enhance employees' skills and knowledge but also boost their morale, productivity, and job satisfaction. In a rapidly evolving business environment, continuous learning and development are crucial for maintaining a competitive edge. Traditional training methods, such as classroom-based instruction, workshops, and on-the-job training, have been the cornerstone of employee development for decades. These methods have proven effective in imparting knowledge and skills, fostering teamwork, and building a cohesive organizational culture. However, they also come with limitations, such as logistical challenges, high costs, and varying levels of engagement among participants.

In recent years, the advent of technology has transformed the landscape of HR practices, including training and development. The integration of digital tools and platforms has enabled organizations to overcome some of the inherent challenges of traditional training methods. Among these technological advancements, Artificial Intelligence (AI) has emerged as a game-changer, offering innovative solutions that enhance the efficiency and effectiveness of training programs.

Introduction to AI-Driven Training Modules

AI-driven training modules represent a cutting-edge approach to employee development, leveraging advanced algorithms and data analytics to deliver personalized and adaptive learning experiences. Unlike traditional training methods, which often follow a one-size-fits-all model, AI-driven modules can tailor content to meet the specific needs and preferences of individual learners. This personalized approach not only enhances engagement but also improves learning retention and skill acquisition.

AI-driven training modules utilize various technologies, including machine learning, natural language processing, and predictive analytics, to create interactive and immersive learning environments. For example, AI can analyze an employee's performance data to identify knowledge gaps and recommend targeted training materials. Similarly, AI-powered chatbots and virtual assistants can provide real-time feedback and support, helping learners to navigate through complex topics and tasks.

The potential benefits of AI-driven training modules extend beyond personalization. These modules can also offer greater flexibility and accessibility, allowing employees to learn at their own pace and convenience. Furthermore, AI can provide valuable insights into the effectiveness of training programs by tracking and analyzing learner progress and outcomes. This data-driven approach enables HR professionals to continuously refine and optimize training strategies, ensuring that they align with organizational goals and objectives.

Despite the promising advantages of AI-driven training, there are also challenges and considerations to address. These include the initial investment in technology infrastructure, potential resistance to change from employees, and ethical concerns related to data privacy and bias. Therefore, a comprehensive evaluation of AI-driven training modules is essential to understand their true impact and potential.

This research paper aims to bridge the gap by analyzing the effectiveness of AI-driven training modules through the lens of demographic factors such as age, qualification, and gender. By examining critical dimensions like engagement, learning retention, user satisfaction, skill development, and cost-effectiveness, the study seeks to provide a comprehensive understanding of how these factors influence the outcomes of AI-driven training. The findings are expected to offer valuable insights for HR professionals and organizational leaders, enabling them to design and implement AI-based training programs that are inclusive and tailored to diverse workforce needs. Ultimately, this research aims to contribute to the broader discourse on the evolving landscape of training and development in the digital age, emphasizing the importance of demographic considerations.

Purpose of the study

The purpose of this study is to evaluate the effectiveness of AI-driven training modules by examining the influence of demographic variables such as age, qualification, and gender. Specifically, the study seeks to assess whether different age groups experience varying levels of engagement, learning retention, skill development, and overall effectiveness when using AI-driven training modules. Additionally, it aims to analyze the impact of educational qualifications to determine if individuals with varying academic backgrounds perceive and benefit from these modules differently in terms of learning outcomes and satisfaction. Furthermore, the study explores whether gender plays a role in shaping the effectiveness of AI-driven training, focusing on aspects such as engagement, adaptability, and learning retention. By investigating these dimensions, the research intends to provide valuable insights for HR professionals and organizational leaders to design inclusive and effective AI-driven training programs that cater to the diverse needs of their workforce.

Literature Review

AI-driven training modules leverage artificial intelligence technologies such as machine learning, natural language processing, and data analytics to provide personalized and adaptive learning experiences. These modules can adjust content in real-time based on individual learner's performance, preferences, and needs. Studies have shown that this level of personalization increases engagement and retention rates among learners (Smith & Johnson, 2020). Moreover, AI-driven training can facilitate continuous learning and development, which is essential in today's fast-paced business environment (Brown et al., 2021).

Traditional training methods, such as classroom-based instruction, workshops, and on-the-job training, have long been the standard for employee development. These methods offer structured learning environments where participants can interact with instructors and peers, facilitating discussion and immediate feedback (Taylor & Green, 2019). Traditional methods are also effective in teaching complex skills that require hands-on practice (Miller & Ross, 2020). However, these methods can be costly and logistically challenging, particularly for large or dispersed workforces.

A comparative study by Wilson and Davis (2021) highlights the strengths and weaknesses of both AI-driven and traditional training methods. While AI-driven training modules provide a high level of customization and scalability, traditional training methods are praised for their ability to foster interpersonal communication and teamwork. The study suggests that a hybrid approach, combining elements of both methods, may offer the best outcomes for employee development (Wilson & Davis, 2021).

Research indicates that AI-driven training modules significantly enhance learning retention by providing tailored feedback and reinforcing learning through adaptive assessments (Nguyen & Lee, 2022). Furthermore, these modules can identify and address individual learning gaps, leading to more effective skill development (Garcia & Martinez, 2021). In contrast, traditional training methods often rely on a one-size-fits-all approach, which may not be as effective in addressing the diverse learning needs of employees.

Implementing AI-driven training programs presents several challenges, including high initial costs, technological infrastructure requirements, and potential resistance from employees accustomed to traditional training methods (Harris & Kim, 2020). Additionally, concerns about data privacy and security are significant, as AI systems often rely on extensive data collection to function effectively (Anderson & Thompson, 2021).

Studies have shown that user satisfaction with AI-driven training modules is generally high due to the personalized learning experience and flexibility offered (Li & Wang, 2021). However, traditional training methods still hold value for their ability to create a sense of community and direct interaction with instructors, which can enhance motivation and engagement (Johnson & Palmer, 2020). A balanced approach that leverages the strengths of both AI-driven and traditional methods may therefore be optimal for maximizing user satisfaction and engagement.

AI-driven training modules can be more cost-effective in the long run due to their scalability and ability to deliver consistent training across large, dispersed workforces (Perez & Gupta, 2022). While the initial setup costs for AI-driven systems can be high, the reduction in travel, venue, and instructor costs can lead to significant savings over time (Robinson & Lewis, 2020). In contrast, traditional training methods often incur ongoing costs related to logistics and materials.

Looking ahead, the integration of AI into training and development is expected to become more sophisticated, with advancements in virtual reality (VR) and augmented reality (AR) further enhancing the learning experience (Chen & Zhao, 2023). These technologies can create immersive, realistic training scenarios that are not possible with traditional methods, providing employees with hands-on experience in a controlled environment.

Research Methodology

Research Design

This study adopts a quantitative research design to evaluate the effectiveness of AI-driven training modules. The approach involves collecting primary data through surveys to measure effectiveness of demographic variables such as age, qualification, and gender engagement, learning retention, user satisfaction, and skill development among employees who have experienced AI driven training modules of training. This design enables a systematic study on effectiveness of AI driven training methods based on participants' feedback and performance metrics.

Population and Sample Size

The population for this study consists of employees from various organizations who have undergone AI-driven training methods. A sample size of 50 participants will be selected using convenience sampling, ensuring that participants will be have experience with training methods. This sample size is adequate to provide preliminary insights and enable statistical analysis of the collected data.

Data Collection Method

Data will be collected through a structured questionnaire designed to capture participants' experiences and perceptions of AI-driven training methods. The questionnaire will consist of 15 questions based on a Likert scale (ranging from 1 to 5, where 1 indicates strong disagreement and 5 indicates strong agreement).

Data Analysis Method

The collected data will be analyzed using various statistical methods to compare the effectiveness of AI-driven training modules. The following tests will be applied:

1)**ANOVA** (one way) for Age & Qualification
2)**T-Test** for Gender

These analyses will help determine the relative effectiveness of AI-driven training modules methods, providing insights into its impact on employee development and organizational performance.

Hypotheses

H1: Different age has different effectiveness while using AI-driven training modules.
H2: There is a significant difference in different qualification while using AI-driven training modules.
H3: There is a significant difference in different gender while using AI-driven training modules.

Questionnaire

The questionnaire will consist of 5 Likert scale questions, ranging from 1 (Strongly Disagree) to 5 (Strongly Agree).

Framework of the Study

Figure: 1

The conceptual framework outlines the key components of the study, focusing on the effectiveness of AI-driven training modules in relation to demographic factors like age, qualification, and gender.

1) Demographic Factors (Age, Qualification, and Gender): These factors are central to the study, exploring how they influence the effectiveness of AI-driven training. The research examines if different age groups, education levels, and genders interact with the training modules in distinct ways.

2) AI-Driven Training Modules: These modules use artificial intelligence to provide personalized learning experiences. The study assesses how these modules impact key learning outcomes, such as engagement, retention, and skill development, considering the influence of demographic factors.

3) Learning Outcomes (Engagement, Retention, Skill Development, Satisfaction, Cost-Effectiveness): The study focuses on how AI training affects engagement, learning retention, skill development, satisfaction, and cost-effectiveness, with demographic factors potentially influencing these outcomes.

4) HR Professionals & Organizational Leaders: The research aims to guide HR professionals and organizational leaders in optimizing training strategies based on demographic insights, ensuring that AI-driven programs are tailored to meet the diverse needs of their workforce.

5) Optimized Training Strategies: The findings will help create more effective and inclusive training programs, enhancing employee development and organizational performance through tailored AI training modules.

This framework highlights how demographic variables can shape the success of AI-driven training and guide organizations in designing more effective, personalized training strategies.

Data Analysis

Univariate Analysis of Variance (ANOVA)

Between-Subjects Factors		N
Age	1.00	4
	2.00	16
	3.00	23
	4.00	8
Qualification	1.00	28
	2.00	12
	3.00	11

Levene's Test of Equality of Error Variances[a,b]		Levene Statistic	df1	df2	Sig.
Effectiveness	Based on Mean	2.333	7	40	.043
	Based on Median	1.411	7	40	.228
	Based on Median and with adjusted df	1.411	7	13.350	.279
	Based on trimmed mean	2.031	7	40	.075
Tests the null hypothesis that the error variance of the dependent variable is equal across groups.					
a. Dependent variable: Effectiveness					
b. Design: Intercept + Age + Qualification + Age * Qualification					

Levene's Test of Equality of Error Variances is utilized to evaluate the uniformity of groups in terms of error variances. The calculated F value is found to be non-significant at the 0.000 levels of significance, which is deemed satisfactory. This finding is crucial when determining the appropriate post hoc test. The decision on the suitable test for groups with differing variances on the test variables will be informed by this result during the selection process.

Tests of Between-Subjects Effects					
Dependent Variable: Effectiveness					
Source	Type III Sum of Squares	df	Mean Square	F	Sig.
Corrected Model	265.552[a]	10	26.555	1.329	.249
Intercept	5021.146	1	5021.146	251.237	.000
Age	137.106	3	45.702	2.287	.093
Qualification	102.111	2	51.056	2.555	.090
Age * Qualification	174.793	5	34.959	1.749	.146
Error	799.429	40	19.986		
Total	10105.000	51			
Corrected Total	1064.980	50			
a. R Squared = .249 (Adjusted R Squared = .062)					

The ANOVA model exhibits a satisfactory fit, as indicated by the adjusted R-squared value of 0.062. The model's goodness of fit was evaluated using an F test, resulting in a noteworthy F value of 1.329 at the 0.249% significance level. The Intercept presents an F value of 251.237, significant at the 0.000% significance level. This implies that 24.9% of errors in the dependent variable are explained, indicating a strong overall model fit. The table above indicates that there is a significant difference in the Effectiveness based on the Age and Qualification of the respondents.

Grand Mean			
Dependent Variable: Effectiveness			
		95% Confidence Interval	
Mean	Std. Error	Lower Bound	Upper Bound
14.481[a]	.890	12.682	16.279
a. Based on modified population marginal mean.			

The mean value is 14.481 with an acceptable standard error of .890. When considering a 95% confidence interval, the lower bound is 12.682 and the upper bound is 16.279.

Post Hoc Tests

Age
H1: Different age has different effectiveness while using AI-driven training modules.

Multiple Comparisons

Dependent Variable: Effectiveness

	(I) Age	(J) Age	Mean Difference (I-J)	Std. Error	Sig.	95% Confidence Interval Lower Bound	95% Confidence Interval Upper Bound
Tukey HSD	1.00	2.00	-.3750	2.49911	.999	-7.0737	6.3237
		3.00	.9348	2.42185	.980	-5.5568	7.4264
		4.00	-.7500	2.73763	.993	-8.0880	6.5880
	2.00	1.00	.3750	2.49911	.999	-6.3237	7.0737
		3.00	1.3098	1.45535	.805	-2.5912	5.2107
		4.00	-.3750	1.93580	.997	-5.5638	4.8138
	3.00	1.00	-.9348	2.42185	.980	-7.4264	5.5568
		2.00	-1.3098	1.45535	.805	-5.2107	2.5912
		4.00	-1.6848	1.83498	.795	-6.6033	3.2337
	4.00	1.00	.7500	2.73763	.993	-6.5880	8.0880
		2.00	.3750	1.93580	.997	-4.8138	5.5638
		3.00	1.6848	1.83498	.795	-3.2337	6.6033
Dunnett t (2-sided)[a]	1.00	4.00	-.7500	2.73763	.984	-7.3831	5.8831
	2.00	4.00	-.3750	1.93580	.994	-5.0653	4.3153
	3.00	4.00	-1.6848	1.83498	.664	-6.1308	2.7613

Based on observed means.

The error term is Mean Square (Error) = 19.986.

a. Dunnett t-tests treat one group as a control, and compare all other groups against it.

Dunnett's t-test reveals insignificant difference between the Groups.

Conclusion: The hypothesis mentioned earlier has been refuted based on the results obtained in the table above.

Effectiveness			
			Subset
	Age	N	1
Tukey HSD[a,b,c]	3.00	23	12.5652
	1.00	4	13.5000
	2.00	16	13.8750
	4.00	8	14.2500
	Sig.		.868
Means for groups in homogeneous subsets are displayed. Based on observed means. The error term is Mean Square (Error) = 19.986.			
a. Uses Harmonic Mean Sample Size = 8.316.			
b. The group sizes are unequal. The harmonic mean of the group sizes is used. Type I error levels are not guaranteed.			
c. Alpha = .05.			

Qualification

H2: There is a significant difference in different qualification while using AI-driven training modules

Multiple Comparisons							
Dependent Variable: Effectiveness							
	(I) Qualification	(J) Qualification	Mean Difference (I-J)	Std. Error	Sig.	95% Confidence Interval Lower Bound	Upper Bound
Tukey HSD	1.00	2.00	-2.8333	1.54248	.171	-6.5876	.9209
		3.00	-.6818	1.59080	.904	-4.5537	3.1901
	2.00	1.00	2.8333	1.54248	.171	-.9209	6.5876
		3.00	2.1515	1.86611	.488	-2.3904	6.6935
	3.00	1.00	.6818	1.59080	.904	-3.1901	4.5537
		2.00	-2.1515	1.86611	.488	-6.6935	2.3904
Dunnett t (2-sided)[a]	1.00	3.00	-.6818	1.59080	.866	-4.3016	2.9380
	2.00	3.00	2.1515	1.86611	.398	-2.0947	6.3977
Based on observed means.							
The error term is Mean Square (Error) = 19.986.							
a. Dunnett t-tests treat one group as a control, and compare all other groups against it.							

Conclusion: The hypothesis (H2) is **rejected** because the results show no significant differences in the effectiveness of AI-driven training modules across different qualifications. The p-values for both Tukey HSD and Dunnett's t-test are not significant (greater than 0.05), indicating that qualification does not have a significant effect on the effectiveness of the AI-driven training modules.

Effectiveness			
		N	Subset 1
	Qualification		1
Tukey HSD[a,b,c]	1.00	28	12.5000
	3.00	11	13.1818
	2.00	12	15.3333
	Sig.		.220
Means for groups in homogeneous subsets are displayed. Based on observed means. The error term is Mean Square (Error) = 19.986.			
a. Uses Harmonic Mean Sample Size = 14.289.			
b. The group sizes are unequal. The harmonic mean of the group sizes is used. Type I error levels are not guaranteed.			
c. Alpha = .05.			

T-Test

H3: There is a significant difference in different gender while using AI-driven training modules.

Group Statistics					
	Gender	N	Mean	Std. Deviation	Std. Error Mean
Effectiveness	1.00	32	13.7188	5.49037	.97057
	2.00	19	12.6316	2.54319	.58345

Independent Samples Test									
		Levene's Test for Equality of Variances		t-test for Equality of Means					
						Sig. (2-tailed)	Mean Difference	Std. Error Difference	95% Confidence Interval of the Difference	
		F	Sig.	t	df				Lower	Upper
Effectiveness	Equal variances assumed	3.814	.057	.811	49	.422	1.08717	1.34126	-1.60820	3.78254
	Equal variances not assumed			.960	46.904	.342	1.08717	1.13244	-1.19112	3.36547

The p-value for the **t-test** is **0.422**, which is much greater than **0.05**. This indicates that the difference between the two gender groups (Male: 1.00, Female: 2.00) in terms of effectiveness is **not statistically significant**.

Confidence Interval of the Difference: The confidence interval for the difference in means (-1.60820 to 3.78254) includes 0, further confirming the lack of a significant difference.

Based on the **t-test** results (p-value = 0.422) and the **confidence interval** that includes zero, **the hypothesis (H3) is rejected**. There is **no significant difference** in the effectiveness of AI-driven training modules between different genders.

Findings: This study evaluated the effectiveness of AI-driven training modules compared to traditional methods, analyzing factors like engagement, learning retention, user satisfaction, skill development, and cost-effectiveness. The findings suggest the following:

1) Engagement and Retention: AI-driven modules exhibit higher engagement and retention rates due to their personalized and adaptive nature.

2) Cost-Effectiveness: While initial implementation costs for AI-driven training are high, the long-term savings outweigh these due to scalability and reduced logistical costs.

3) Demographic Analysis: Age and qualification showed no significant differences in effectiveness, and gender-based analysis revealed no substantial variation in outcomes.

4) Overall Performance: Both methods have unique advantages; traditional methods excel in interpersonal and hands-on learning, while AI-driven modules lead in flexibility and scalability.

Results of Tests and Hypotheses

The study tested three hypotheses through ANOVA and T-tests:

1) **H1 (Age and Effectiveness):** Rejected, as no significant differences were found in the effectiveness of AI-driven training modules across different age groups.

2) **H2 (Qualification and Effectiveness):** Rejected, as the analysis indicated no significant differences in effectiveness based on participants' qualifications.

3)**H3 (Gender and Effectiveness):** Rejected, with no statistically significant differences observed in the effectiveness of AI-driven training modules between male and female participants.

These results highlight the broad applicability of AI-driven training modules across diverse demographics, making them a viable option for varied organizational settings.

Conclusion

This study evaluated the effectiveness of AI-driven training modules with a specific focus on the impact of demographic factors, such as age, qualification, and gender, on key aspects of employee development, including engagement, learning retention, user satisfaction, skill development, and cost-effectiveness. The findings indicate that AI-driven modules significantly enhance engagement and retention due to their personalized and adaptive nature. Despite higher initial implementation costs, these modules are more cost-effective over time due to their scalability and reduced logistical expenses.

However, demographic analysis revealed no significant differences in the effectiveness of AI-driven training across age groups, qualifications, or gender, as tested through ANOVA and T-tests. This suggests that AI-driven modules exhibit universal applicability across diverse demographic profiles. While traditional training methods may be more effective in fostering interpersonal skills and hands-on learning, AI-driven modules excel in offering flexibility, personalization, and data-driven adaptability, indicating that a hybrid approach combining both methods could optimize training outcomes.

These results have important implications for HR practices, emphasizing the value of AI-driven training in personalizing learning and improving employee satisfaction. Future research should address the limitations of this study, including sample size, industry-specific factors, and technological biases. Additionally, ethical concerns regarding data privacy and algorithmic bias should be explored to ensure responsible integration of AI in organizational training programs. Ultimately, this study lays a foundation for understanding how AI-driven training can enhance employee development across various demographic groups, highlighting the need for further investigation into its potential and challenges.

References

1) Anderson, P., & Thompson, G. (2021). Data privacy in AI-driven training systems. Cybersecurity Journal, 19(2), 58-73.

2)Brown, P., et al. (2021). Continuous learning through AI: Transforming the workplace. Workforce Development Journal, 38(4), 89-102.

3)Chen, Y., & Zhao, L. (2023). The future of AI in training: VR and AR applications. *Journal of Future Technologies*, 37(1), 45-60.

4)Garcia, L., & Martinez, R. (2021). Skill development in the age of AI: A new paradigm. Training and Development Quarterly, 27(4), 150-168.

5)Harris, J., & Kim, S. (2020). Overcoming challenges in AI-driven training implementation. Journal of Business Technology, 33(3), 112-126.

6)Johnson, M., & Palmer, K. (2020). The role of community in traditional training methods. HR Management Journal, 22(3), 187-199.

7)Li, J., & Wang, H. (2021). User satisfaction in AI-driven learning environments. Journal of Educational Research, 58(1), 92-104.

8)Miller, S., & Ross, D. (2020). Hands-on learning in the workplace: The value of traditional training methods. Journal of Business Training, 34(3), 201-215.

9)Nguyen, T., & Lee, C. (2022). AI in education: Improving learning retention through adaptive technologies. Educational Research and Development Journal, 41(1), 67-84.

10)Perez, A., & Gupta, N. (2022). Cost-benefit analysis of AI-driven training systems. Financial Management Review, 46(2), 134-149.

11)Robinson, T., & Lewis, P. (2020). Economic advantages of AI in employee training. Journal of Business Economics, 28(4), 203-218.

12)Smith, J., & Johnson, A. (2020). The impact of AI on

personalized learning experiences. Journal of Educational Technology, 45(2), 123-135.

13)Taylor, R., & Green, K. (2019). The role of traditional training in skill development. HR Training and Development Review, 29(1), 45-58.

14) Wilson, L., & Davis, M. (2021). Comparing AI-driven and traditional training methods: A hybrid approach. *Journal of Organizational Learning*, 50(2), 98-112.

Web-links

1)https://www.researchgate.net/publication/ 373424876_The_Impact_of_AI- Driven_Personalization_on_Learners'_Performance
2)https://www.researchgate.net/publication/ 377366571_Impact_of_Artificial_Intelligence_Versus_Tradional_ Instruction_f
3)https://www.ncbi.nlm.nih.gov/pmc/articles/PMC8865945/
4)https://www.sciencedirect.com/science/article/pii/ S2451958822000574

CHAPTER IV

"The Role of Psychological Contract in Retention Management"

Dr. Shraddha Upadhyay
(Assistant. Professor - Graduate School of Business, Indore)

Abstract

Today's growing "war for talent" is making it more and more difficult for organizations to keep current employees and to find qualified replacements. This study examines the challenges that organizations face with employee retention in an increasingly competitive labor market.

This article examines employees' views on the factors affecting employee retention. This is done by integrating findings from the literature on retention management with the theoretical framework of the psychological contract. In this study, respondents from a diverse group of private organizations described the factors they believed to affect employee retention and the retention practices set up in their organization. Employees were asked to report on the importance attached to four types of employer inducements commonly regarded as retention factors. They also evaluated their employers' delivery of these inducements and provided information on their loyalty; intentions to stay and job search behaviors. The results of the study are discussed and implications for HR managers are highlighted.

Introduction

Both researchers and human resource (HR) practitioners agree that the employment relationship is undergoing fundamental changes that have implications for the attraction, motivation and retention of talented employees (Horwitz, Heng, & Quazi, 2003: Roehling, Cavanaugh, Moyhihan & Boswell, 2000; Turnley & Feldman, 2000). Over the past decades, the economic environment has been changed dramatically. Due to on-going evolutions towards international competition and globalization of markets, organizations are required to be more flexible and to increase their productivity. This has reduced the job security of employees at all levels in the organization (King, 2000) but at the same time HR managers are pressed to attract and retain talented employees who have competencies that are critical for organizational survival (Horwitz et al., 2003; Mitchell, Holtom & Lee, 2001; Roehling et al., 2000; Steel, Griffeth & Hom, 2002). Often, however, these employees are difficult to retain due to their tendency to attach more importance to marking out their own career path than to organizational loyalty; a tendency which results in increased rates of voluntary turnover (Cappelli, 2001). Within the HRM literature, retention management has become a popular concept to examine the portfolio of HR practices put into place by organizations in order to reduce voluntary turnover rates (e.g. Cappelli, 2001; Mitchell et al., 2001; Steel et al., 2002).

Another concept that has gained interest as a construct relevant for understanding and managing contemporary employment relationships is the psychological contract, which refers to employees' subjective interpretations and evaluations of their deal with the organization (Rousseau, 1996; 2001; Turnley & Feldman, 1998). Researchers in this field argue that in order for retention management to be effective, the creation of an optimal portfolio of HR practices is not sufficient and that it is important to manage employees' expectations relating to these practices. Only in this way HR managers can be confident to create a deal that is mutually understood by both the organization and its employees (Rousseau, 1996).

HR Factors Affecting Employee Retention

In view of the large costs associated with employee turnover, even in a Global Economic Downturn, characterized by downsizing and layoffs, HR managers still need to work out HR practices that enable them to retain their talented employees (Horwitz et al., 2003; Steel et al., 2002). These practices are often bundled under the term "retention management". Retention management is defined as "the ability to hold onto those employees you want to keep, for longer than your competitors" (Johnson, 2000). In the literature numerous factors are put forward as important in affecting employee retention, varying from purely financial inducements to so-called "new-age" benefits. These inducements can be grouped into four major categories of retention factors, namely (1) financial incentives, (2) career development opportunities, (3) job content, (4) social atmosphere, and work-life balance (e.g. Horwich et al., 2003; Roehling et al., 2000; Ulrich, 1998).

First, financial rewards, or the provision of an attractive remuneration package, are one of the most widely discussed retention factors, since they not only fulfill financial and material needs. They also have a social meaning, with the salary level providing an indication of the employee's relative position of power and status within the organization. However, research shows that there is much inter individual variability in the importance of financial rewards for employee retention (Pfeffer, 1998; Woodruffe, 1999). For instance, a study conducted by the "Institute for Employment Studies" (Bevan, 1997) reveals that only ten percent of people who had left their employer gave dissatisfaction with pay as the main reason for leaving. However, despite the fact.

That many studies show financial rewards to be a poor motivating factor, it remains a tactic used by many organizations to commit their employees to the organization by means of remuneration Packages (Cappelli, 2001; Mitchell et al., 2001; Woodruffe, 1999). For instance, in a recent study Horwitzet al. (2003) found that the most popular retention strategies reported by HR managers of knowledge firms still related to compensation.

Second, opportunities for career development are considered as one of the most important factors affecting employee retention. It is suggested that a company that wants to strengthen its bond with its employees must invest in the development of these employees (Hall & Moss, 1998; Hsu, Jiang, Klein & Tang, 2003; Steel et al., 2002; Woodruffe, 1999). Other factors relating to career development are the provision of mentoring or coaching to employees, the organization of career management workshops and the setup of competency management programs (Roehling et al., 2000). For instance, in a recent study Allen, Shore & Griffeth (2003) found that employees 'perceptions of growth opportunities offered by their employer reduced turnover intentions. Steel et al. (2002) also report empirical data showing that lack of training and promotional opportunities were the most frequently cited reason for high-performers to leave the company.

The third category of retention factors relates to employees' job content, more specifically the provision of challenging and meaningful work. It builds on the assumption that people do not just work for the money but also to create purpose and satisfaction in their life (Mitchell et al., 2001; Pfeffer, 1998). According to Woodruffe (1999) employees, in addition to a strong need to deliver excellent results, also want to take on difficult challenges that are relevant for the organization. However, when their work mainly consists of the routine-based performance of tasks, the likelihood of de-motivation and turnover is relatively high. By thinking carefully about which tasks to include in which jobs, companies can affect their retention rates (Steel et al., 2002). The social atmosphere, i.e. the work environment and the social ties within this environment, is the fourth retention factor considered by many researchers. Cappelli (2001) states that loyalty to the organization is a thing of the past, but that loyalty to one's colleagues acts as an effective means of retention. When an employee decides to leave the organization, this also means the loss of a social network. Some research suggests that social contacts between colleagues and department are an important factor for retaining talent. Organizations can contribute to the creation of a positive social atmosphere by stimulating interaction and mutual cooperation among colleagues and through open and honest communication between management and employees (Roehling et al., 2000).

The conflict between work and career on the one hand and private life on the other is currently assuming large proportions in our society. There is an increasing demand for more flexible forms of work, which would positively affect the reduction of the work-family conflict and employee satisfaction in general (Anderson et al., 2002; Kossek & Ozeki, 1998). HR policies addressing work-life balance are assumed to be important because the current generation of employees attaches much importance to quality of life, as a result of the ever increasing work pressure (Cappelli, 2001; Mitchell et al., 2001). Research suggests that policies aimed at improving the work-life balance are successful if they are implemented in a supportive context that truly allows employees to make meaningful and useful choices (Anderson et al., 2002: Kossek & Ozeki, 1998).

Impact of the Psychological Contract on Employee Retention

Many researchers argue that the psychological contract plays an important role in helping to define and understand the contemporary employment relationship (Rousseau, 2001; Shore &

Coyle-Shapiro, 2003; Turnley & Feldman, 1998). Psychological contracts consist of individuals' beliefs regarding the terms and conditions of the exchange agreement between themselves and their organizations (Rousseau, 1996).

They emerge when individuals believe that their organization has promised to provide them with certain inducements in return for the contributions they make to the organization (Turnley & Feldman, 2000). The growing body of literature on the psychological contract reflects accumulating evidence for its influence on diverse work-related outcomes. These studies show that employees evaluate the inducements they receive from their organization in view of previously made promises and that this evaluation leads to a feeling of psychological contract fulfillment or breach (Turnley & Feldman, 1998). In turn, a feeling of contract breach has a negative impact on employees' willingness to contribute to the organization and on their intentions to stay with the organization (e.g. Coyle-Shapiro, 2002; Robinson, 1996; Robinson, Kraatz & Rousseau; Turnley & Feldman, 1998; 2000). Other studies have found a positive correlation with actual turnover (e.g. Guzzo, Noonan & Elron, 1994; Robinson, 1996). Together these results suggest that the psychological contract is a construct of both scientific and practical importance and that it is especially relevant for HR managers concerned with the retention of their employees.

Existing research indicates that employees are rather pessimistic about the extent to which their organization lives up to its promises. For example, Turnley & Feldman (1998) found that approximately twenty-five percent of their sample of employees felt that they had received less (or much less) than they had been promised. This was most strongly the case for promises relating to job security, amount of input into important decisions, opportunities for advancement, health care benefits, and responsibility and power. Robinson et al. (1994) found that fifty-five percent of their sample reported contract violations by their employer two years after organizational entry. . Together, this empirical work demonstrates that psychological contract violation is relatively common and that this could explain the difficulties organizations are currently experiencing in retaining their employees Since the psychological contract encompasses employees' subjective interpretations and evaluations of their employment deal, the retention factors discussed in the practitioner and scientific literature will only turn out to be effective for employee retention if they are in line with employees' subjective views and expectations.

Objectives of the Study

The factors which are important for Retaining talents in organization such as opportunities for promotion ,the development of the people and to create a positive social atmosphere by stimulating interaction and mutual cooperation among the employees.

Research Methodology

Design & Sampling

The sample of the present study consisted of N=200 employees from Private Organizations. Stratified random technique was used for data collection. The research was carried out through survey method with the help of self-developed structured, non-disguised questionnaire. It consisted of statements based on 5 point Likert scale .Employees was asked to give their opinion for the questions given in the questionnaire. This evaluation was related to employees' loyalty, their intentions to leave the company and their job search behaviors.

We refer to five retention factors discussed in the theoretical part of this paper:

1. Financial rewards (e.g. "an attractive pay and benefits package")
2. Career development (e.g. "opportunities for promotion")
3. Job content (e.g. "a job with responsibilities")
4. Social atmosphere (e.g. "good mutual cooperation"
5. Work-life balance (e.g. "respect for your personal situation").
Each dimension was assessed by five items.

Hypothesis:

Here we create 3 null hypotheses.

Ho: there is no impact of financial rewards on career development.
Ho: there is no impact of job content on work balance.
Ho: there is no impact of social atmosphere on work balance.

Results and Discussions

(Please See Table)

On the basis of the table we conclude that the difference between mean values is less than 1.96 times S.E. so we reject our null hypothesis at 1% level of significance. that means we can say that the factors which are important for Retaining talents in organization such as opportunities for promotion ,the development of the people and to create a positive social atmosphere by stimulating interaction and mutual cooperation among the employees. That means there is a positive impact on different factors in retention management.

Earlier studies have depicted that both practitioners and researchers in the field of retention management agree that creating a retention policy that works is not an easy task. One of the first and necessary steps in working out a retention policy for HR is to assess the retention factors which are important to their workforce (Steel et al., 2002). The collection of targeted data on reasons for quitting and staying, segmented by employee groups (e.g. male versus female, blue collar versus white collar) is an important means for obtaining this information… For example, while social atmosphere is mentioned as a major reason for staying, it is not considered to be an important reason for voluntary turnover. Inversely, inducements relating to work-life balance are cited as a reason for voluntary turnover but not as a reason for staying.

In general, it appears that retention practices are more focused on the factors which are believed to cause employee turnover rather than on those believed to affect employee retention. This Focuses on career opportunities and financial inducements. Although compensation matters, employees are more concerned with the level of fulfillment they get from their jobs. They also feel that working with an understanding supervisor or manager in a cooperative and trusting work environment is important. Organizations should focus on making sure that the people they hire are a good match for the job and the work culture.

The evaluation of promises about career opportunities appears to be most predictive of employees' intentions to leave and of their job search behaviors and they are also strongly predictive of employee loyalty. This finding is in line with HR managers' views that career development is an important factor affecting both voluntary employee turnover and retention and it supports their efforts to work out retention policies focusing on career development.

An employee's relationship with his or her supervisor or manager and work-life balance are the most important determinants for staying with an organization. Senior leaders should be encouraged to succession plan which is another tool to motivate employees to keep developing. Management teams need to be educated in succession planning concepts and can be motivated by having succession planning included as a performance criterion. Failure to develop successors may prevent them achieving higher career objectives themselves.

Employers need to anticipate what their expectations will be of employees in the future to ensure that they create a realistic job description .Organizations must also focus on employee engagement to ensure that their workforce is committed to the long-term success of their organization and want to stay with the organization to honor this commitment. Engaged employees will also act as ambassadors and produce better results.

Managerial Implications

Why an employee stays with the organization is a strategic issue for HR managers as well as a major concern for the individual. Having insight into those factors most important in determining employee retention is important for HR managers in order to work out retention policies and practices that are effective both at the individual and the organizational level. Taken together, the results of our employee survey indicate that career development is the most important retention factor since offering good opportunities for career development not only prevents employees from leaving the company, but it also contributes in a positive way to their loyalty to the firm. If we assume that the aim of retention policies is not only to retain employees but also to retain employees who are loyal and committed, then HR managers must also put more efforts in retention policies relating to the social atmosphere and to job content. Both factors are important predictors of employee loyalty and they also significantly prevent employees from leaving their organization. On the other hand, the results relating to work-life balance and financial rewards, the two factors that can be considered more as extrinsic rather than intrinsic rewards, suggest that retention policies focusing only on these factors might be little effective. Employees' evaluations of organizational inducements about work-life balance consistently have no significant impact on their loyalty, intentions to stay or job search behaviors and thus should not be considered as important retention factors.

The main message we derive from this study is that HR managers should better take into account what their employees value and how they evaluate their organization's efforts towards retention management if they are to contribute in a cost-efficient way to the strategic objectives of the organization. The psychological contract hereby provides a practically useful framework to manage employees' expectations and to engage in an open process of communication and negotiation about the employment deal (Herriot & Pemberton, 1996). If HR managers are to be effective in their retention management this means that they should take into account this subjectivity instead of departing from generally agreed-upon views on what's important to employees in general. This, in turn, should contribute to their role in the company as a strategic partner given that the attraction and retention of talented employees will stay an important factor of competitive advantage for organizations, both in times of economic downturn and upheaval.

References

1. Allen, D. G., Shore, L. M., & Griffeth, R. W. (2003). The role of perceived organizational support and supportive human resource practices in the turnover process. Journal of Management, 29(1), 99-118.
2. Anderson, S. E., Coffey, B. S., & Byerly, R. T. (2002). Formal organizational initiatives and formal workplace practices: Links to work-family conflict and job-related outcomes. Journal of Management, 28(6), 787-810.
3. Bevan S., 1997, Quit stalling, People Management, november, 32-35.
4. Bluedorn, A. C. (1982). A unified model of turnover from organizations. Human Relations, 35(2), 135-153.

5. Boroff, K.E., & Lewin, D. (1997). Loyalty, voice, and intent to exit a union firm: A conceptual and empirical analyses. Industrial and Labor Relations Review, 51(1), 50-63.

6. Butler, T. en Waldroop, J. (2001). Job sculpting: The art of retaining your best people. 7.Harvard Business Review on finding and keeping the best people (pp. 179-203). Boston: Harvard Business School Press.

8. Cappelli, P. (2001). A market-driven approach to retaining talent. Harvard Business Review on finding and keeping the best people (pp. 27-50). Boston: Harvard Business School Press.

9. Coyle-Shapiro, J. A.-M. (2002). A psychological contract perspective on organizational citizenship behavior. Journal of Organizational Behavior, 23(8), 927-946.

10. De Vos, A. (2002). The individual antecedents and the development of newcomers' psychological contracts during the socialization process: A longitudinal study. Doctoral dissertation, Faculty of Economics and Business Adminstration, Ghent University.

11. De Vos, A., & Buelens, M. (2004). Differences between private and public sector employees' psychological contracts. Manuscript under review.

12. De Vos, A., Buyens, D, & Schalk, R. (2003). Psychological contract development during organizational socialization: Adaptation to reality and the role of reciprocity. Journal of Organizational Behavior, 24(5), 537-599.

13. Guzzo, R. A., Noonan, K. A., & Elron, E. (1994). Expatriate managers and the psychological contract. Journal of Applied Psychology, 79(4), 617-626.

14. Hall, D. T., & Moss, J. E. (1998). The new protean career contract: Helping organizations and employees adapt. Organisational Dynamics, 26(3), 22-37.

15. Herriot, P., & Pemberton, C. (1996). Contracting careers. Human Relations, 49(6), 757-790.

16. Horwitz, F. M., Heng, C. T., & Quazi, H. A. (2003). Finders, keepers? Attracting, motivating and retaining knowledge workers.

Human Resource Management Journal, 13(4), 23-44.

17. Hsu, M. K., Jiang, J. J., Klein, G., & Tang, Z. (2003). Perceived career incentives and intent to leave. Information & Management, 40, 361-369.

18. Johnson M., 2000, Winning the people wars, talent and the battle for human capital. London, UK: Copyright Licensing Agency.

19. King, J. E. (2000). White-collar reactions to job insecurity and the role of the psychological contract: Implications for human resource management. Human Resource Management, 39(1), 79-92.

20. Kopelman, R. E., Rovenpor, J. L., & Millsap, R. E. (1992). Rationale and construct validity evidence for the Job Search Behavior Index: Because intentions (and New Year's resolutions) often come to naught. Journal of Vocational Behavior, 40, 269-287.

21. Kossek, E. E., & Ozeki, C. (1998). Work-family conflict, policies, and the job-life satisfaction relationship: A review and directions for organizational behavior – human resources research. Journal of Applied Psychology, 83, 139-149.

22. Mitchell, T. R., Holtom, B.C., & Lee, T. W. (2001). How to keep your best employees Developing an effective retention policy. Academy of Management Executive, 15(4), 96-109.

Pfeffer J., 1998, Six myths about pay, Harvard Business Review, May-June, 38-57.

23. Robinson, S. L. (1996). Trust and breach of the psychological contract. Administrative Science Quarterly, 41, 574-599.

24. Robinson, S. L., Kraatz, M. S., & Rousseau, D. M. (1994). Changing obligations and the psychological contract: A longitudinal study. Academy of Management Journal, 37(1), 137-152.

25. Roehling, M. V., Cavanaugh, M. A., Moynihan, L. M., & Boswell, W. (2000). The nature of the new employment relationship: A content analysis of the practitioner and academic literatures. Human Resource Management, 39(4), 305-320.

26. Rousseau, D. M. (1996). Changing the deal while keeping the people. Academy of Management Executive, 10(1), 50-58.

27. Rousseau, D. M. (2001). The idiosyncratic deal: Flexibility

versus fairness? Organizational Dynamics, 29(4), 260-273.

28. Shore, L. M., & Coyle-Shapiro, J. A.-M. (2003). Editorial. New developments in the employee-organization relationship. Journal of Organizational Behavior, 24, 443-450.

29. Steel, R. P., Griffeth, R. W., & Hom, P. W. (2002). Practical retention policy for the practical manager. Academy of Management Executive, 18(2), 149-16 9.

30. Turnley, W. H., & Feldman, D. C. (1998). Psychological contract violation during corporate restructuring. Human Resource Management, 37(1), 71-83.

31. Turnley, W. H., & Feldman, D. C. (2000). Re-examining the effects of psychological contract violations: unmet expectations and job dissatisfaction as mediators. Journal of Organizational Behavior, 1- 21, 25-42.

Table for Z-test

	Financial rewards & career development		Job content & social atmosphere		Social atmosphere & work life balance	
N = 200	Mean	S.E.	Mean	S.E.	Mean	S.E.
	2.2	4.2	2.7	3.8	2.9	7.2

"Bridging the Gap: Strategies for Integrating Skill–Based Education in Higher Education through Industry Collaboration to Enhance Employability"

Dr. Sonali Solanki
(Assistant Professor, St. Paul Institute of Professional Studies (Autonomous), Indore)
Dr. Danish Khan
(Assistant Professor, St. Paul Institute of Professional Studies (Autonomous), Indore)

Abstract

This study examines approaches for incorporating skill-based education into higher education by fostering collaboration with industries, with the goal of improving the employability of graduates. Some important methods include collaborating with industry professionals to develop educational programs, increasing opportunities for internships and apprenticeships, promoting exchanges between professors and industry, and incorporating certification programs. The focus is on integrating training for soft skills, investing in cutting-edge technology, and promoting collaborative research initiatives. The study emphasizes the significance of on-going feedback mechanisms and resilient career services in order to sustain relevance and efficacy. These initiatives ensure that graduates are adequately equipped to fulfil the requirements of the contemporary workforce by connecting academia and industry.

Introduction

In recent years, the incorporation of skill-based education in higher education institutions has emerged as a critical strategy for improving the employability of graduates. The conventional educational system, which emphasizes theoretical knowledge, frequently fails to provide students with the practical skills that are necessary in the workplace. The labor market can be significantly mismatched as a result of this discrepancy between academic knowledge and industry requirements, which can impact the productivity of industries and the employability of graduates (John & Doe, 2020).

Integrating skill-focused education into higher education is crucial in order to adequately equip graduates with the practical skills and competences that employers highly prioritize, thereby increasing their chances of success in the competitive labor market. By incorporating these tactics, establishments can cultivate an educational setting that amplifies pupils' job prospects and equips them for triumph in their careers. Higher education institutions have designed vocational and elective courses in response to industry demands, ensuring that students acquire practical skills that are directly relevant to their chosen professions. The effective incorporation of skill-based education through industrial partnership not only improves the job prospects of graduates but also promotes innovation and economic expansion. By investing in education, industries can acquire a more skilled and capable staff, leading to technical progress and enhanced production (White, 2018).

In order to tackle this problem, many educational institutions and corporations are investigating collaborative approaches. These approaches strive to synchronize educational curriculum with the ever-changing demands of the work market. For example, the inclusion of internships, apprenticeships, as well as industry-led projects in academic programs has demonstrated encouraging outcomes in closing this divide (Smith, 2019). Moreover, the direct participation of industry experts in designing and implementing the curriculum helps provide students with current and applicable expertise and understanding (Brown & Green, 2021).

Important elements and approaches for incorporating skill-based education in higher education encompass the identification of pertinent skills, the integration of skills into the curriculum, the provision of experiential learning opportunities, and the cultivation of project-based learning. Additional significant approaches include industry partnership, skill evaluation and certification, professional growth, technology incorporation, feedback and on-going enhancement, and faculty advancement. The aim of incorporating skill-based education into higher education through industry collaboration is to close the disparity between academic learning and industry demands, hence improving students' job prospects. The objective of this research study is to discover efficient approaches for incorporating skill-based education into higher education curricula by collaborating with industry partners. Furthermore, to determine the influence of skill-based education and industrial partnership on the employability of graduates.

Review of Literature

The incorporation of skill-oriented education into higher education through partnership with industries is increasingly seen as crucial for improving the employability of graduates.

Husu (2019) contends that engaging industry stakeholders in collaborative curriculum design ensures that educational programs are in sync with prevailing market trends and demands. This technique guarantees that graduates acquire pertinent skills that are in high demand by businesses.

Lasonen (2016) highlights the importance of collaborations among higher education establishments and industry in influencing curriculum material and delivery, hence improving the practical relevance of education to real-life situations. Ongoing feedback methods are essential for assessing and improving skill-based education projects.

Morrison et al. (2018) argue that feedback from employers, alumni, and industry experts is a vital source of information for evaluating the performance of educational programs. This feedback helps identify essential changes to ensure that the programs align with the changing demands of the business.

Zegwaard et al. (2017) also emphasize the significance of continuous feedback loops in ensuring that educational curricula remain relevant and responsive to the needs of the business. The empirical study emphasizes the favorable results of educational activities that are connected to the industry on the employability of graduates.

Gribble et al. (2018) and Yorke & Knight (2004) have discovered that graduates who engage in internships, apprenticeships, and industry projects exhibit elevated levels of employment and progression in their careers. These events serve to both connect academic learning with practical skills and improve graduates' preparedness for the competitive labor market.

Ultimately, it is crucial to utilize industrial collaboration in order to include skill-based education into higher education, as this is vital for equipping graduates with the necessary tools to thrive in their professional endeavors. This literature review consolidates evidence that supports the use of collaborative curriculum design, continuous feedback systems, and industry-linked training activities to improve employability outcomes.

Research Methodology

The current study uses a descriptive study methodology to examine methods for incorporating skill-based education in higher education by collaborating with industries to improve job prospects. The methodology relies mainly on secondary data obtained from a variety of published articles, research studies, journals, and reliable websites.

Strategies for Integrating Skill-Based Education in Higher Education

In order to incorporate skill-based education into higher education through industrial engagement, various ways can be employed to improve employability:

1. Curriculum Co-Design: Engage in collaborative efforts with industry professionals to develop and enhance curricula that are in line with present industry standards and anticipated skill requirements. This guarantees that students acquire pertinent and pragmatic competencies that can be promptly utilized in professional settings (Smith, 2020).

2. Internships and Apprenticeships: Create well-organized internship and apprenticeship initiatives in collaboration with industry associations. These programs offer students practical experience, enhancing their appeal to prospective employers (Jones, 2019).

3. Industry-Led Workshops and Seminars: Arrange workshops and seminars conducted by experts from the industry to provide students with valuable knowledge about the practical applications of their studies and the latest developments in the industry (Brown & Adams, 2018).

4. Faculty Exchange Programs: Implement faculty exchange programs that involve industry professionals instructing courses or leading training sessions, while academic faculty members acquire first-hand experience in the field. This reciprocal interchange enhances the educational experience and guarantees the pertinence of teaching methodologies and subject matter (White, 2017).

5. Collaborative Research initiatives: Involve students in research initiatives that tackle genuine industrial concerns. These initiatives have the potential to stimulate innovation and offer students valuable opportunities to develop practical problem-solving skills (Miller et al., 2021).

6. Certification Programs: Collaborate with the industry to provide certification programs that are acknowledged and highly esteemed by employers. These certifications can be included into the degree programs, offering students supplementary qualifications (Johnson, 2022).

7. Career Services and Networking: Enhance career services through the establishment of industry collaborations that provide networking opportunities, job fairs, and professional guidance. Students can develop valuable professional networks and get valuable knowledge about the job market through this (Davis & Clark, 2019).

8. Technology and Resource Sharing: Engage in partnerships with the industry to gain access to state-of-the-art technology and resources that may not be accessible within the academic institution. By providing access to cutting-edge equipment and software, students are able to receive training on the most up-to-date tools shnd technologies used in their respective disciplines (Wilson, 2020).

By employing these measures, higher education institutions can successfully close the divide between academic learning and industry requirements, thus improving the job prospects of its graduates.

Impact of skill-based education and industrial collaboration on the employability of graduates

1. Relevance of Skills: Skill-based education aims to provide students with practical skills that have direct relevance and applicability in professional settings. Through collaboration with industries, educational institutions may ensure that the skills they teach are up-to-date and highly sought-after, precisely matching the needs of the sector. This enhances the desirability of graduates for businesses who are seeking candidates who are prepared to make an immediate impact.

2. Industry Exposure: Partnerships between educational institutions and industry offer students the opportunity to gain first-hand experience in authentic situations, difficulties, and methodologies. The exposure can encompass internships, cooperative programs, industry-sponsored initiatives, and guest lectures delivered by industry leaders. These experiences not only enrich students' comprehension but also provide them with a glimpse of the professional setting, enhancing their preparedness for employment.

3. Employability Skills: In addition to technical skills, partnership with industries also prioritizes the cultivation of employability skills such as effective communication, seamless teamwork, and proficient problem-solving and flexible adaptability. These abilities are vital for achieving success in any work and are frequently mentioned by employers as indispensable criteria throughout the hiring process.

4. Networking Opportunities: Industrial partnership frequently enables students to access networking opportunities. By establishing professional relationships, students have the opportunity to secure work possibilities prior to completing their studies. Networking is a potent weapon in the job market and can greatly improve the employability of graduates.

5. Curriculum Enhancement: Educational institutions can periodically update their curriculum by collaborating with enterprises to incorporate technological breakthroughs, industry trends, and growing skills requirements. This guarantees that graduates are thoroughly equipped with the most up-to-date knowledge and skills, hence minimizing the disparity between academic education and industry requirements.

6. Higher Job Placement Rates: Programs that prioritize skill-based education and have robust corporate partnerships tend to yield higher percentages of job placement for their graduates. Employers highly appreciate applicants who have practical skills and can make immediate and valuable contributions, resulting in faster and more successful transitions from college to employment.

Conclusion

Facilitating the connection between higher education and industry via skill-based education is crucial for augmenting the employability of graduates. Higher education institutions may assure the relevance and alignment of their curricula with the demands of the modern workforce by establishing strategic alliances with industry. Structured internships and apprenticeships offer hands-on experience, while industry-led workshops, certification programs, and investments in technology give students with state-of-the-art capabilities. Faculty-industry exchanges and collaborative research initiatives enrich the learning experience, promoting a culture of innovation and practical problem-solving.

Furthermore, it is essential to enhance career services and integrate soft skills training into academic programs in order to adequately equip students for prosperous professions. Institutions can ensure prolonged relevance and effectiveness by implementing continuous feedback systems and evaluating outcomes to adjust and enhance their tactics. By making these collaborative endeavors, higher education institutions may generate graduates who possess not just strong academic skills but also the capacity to effectively navigate the ever-changing job market. This will greatly improve their chances of finding employment and advancing in their careers.

References:

1. Bano, Y., & Vasantha, S. (2019). Review on strategies for bridging the employability skill Gapin higher education. International Journal of Recent Technology and Engineering, 7(6S5), 1147-1152.
2. Brown, J., & Green, L. (2021). Enhancing employability: The role of industry in higher education. Journal of Higher Education Policy, 35(2), 123-145.
3. Bridgstock, R. (2016). Skills for creative industries graduate success. Education + Training, 58(1), 43-59.
4. Cranmer, S. (2006). Employability skills for the future. Higher Education Academy. Retrieved from https://www.heacademy.ac.uk/knowledge-hub/employability-skills-future
5. Gribble, C., Blackmore, J., Rahimi, M., & Davies, A. (2018). Fostering graduate employability: Partnerships for a future-ready workforce. Higher Education Research & Development, 37(3), 561-575.
6. Harvey, L., Moon, S., & Geall, V. (2018). Graduates' work: Organisational change and students' attributes. Studies in Higher Education, 43(9), 1538-1553.
7. Husu, J. (2019). Curriculum alignment in higher education: A systematic review of literature. Teaching in Higher Education,

24(7), 837-857.

8. John, R., & Doe, M. (2020). The skills gap: Challenges and solutions in the 21st century. Educational Review, 42(3), 245-267.

9. Johnson, E. (2022). Certification Programs: Enhancing Graduate Employability. Professional Development Quarterly, 19(3), 67-85.

10. Knight, P. T., & Yorke, M. (2003). Employability and good learning in higher education. Teaching in Higher Education, 8(1), 3-16.

11. Lasonen, J. (2016). Curricula and collaboration: Fostering excellence and employability in higher education. Journal of Education and Work, 29(4), 401-419.

12. Morrison, M., & Bennett, R. (2018). Evaluating the employability skills gap: How can we better prepare graduates for the workplace? Higher Education Research & Development, 37(7), 1435-1449.

13. Mullen, C. A., & Preston, A. E. (2013). The effects of internships on college student academic performance. Economic Inquiry, 51(1), 406-419.

14. Pilbeam, C., & Tuck, J. (2015). Collaboration between higher education and industry: Employability skills for engineers. European Journal of Engineering Education, 40(6), 583-601.

15. Sarin, C. (2019). Analyzing skill gap between higher education and employability. Research Journal of Humanities and Social Sciences, 10(3), 941-948.

16. Sharma, I., & Sharma, I. (2021). Integrating Skill-Based Education In Indian Higher Education Sector: Transitioning From Academia To Workplace. Towards Excellence, 13(2).

17. Smith, A. (2019). Bridging theory and practice: Internship programs in higher education. Vocational Education Journal, 30(1), 78-90.

18. White, T. (2018). The economic impact of skill-based education. Industrial and Labor Relations Review, 71(4), 845-869.

19. Yorke, M., & Knight, P. T. (2004). Embedding employability into the curriculum. Higher Education Academy.

https://www.heacademy.ac.uk/knowledge-hub/embedding-
employability-curriculum.

CHAPTER VI

"Utilizing AI for the Growth of Management Institutions"

Prof. (Dr.) Manisha Pandey
(Professor, SCMR & HOD, R&D Cell, ITM University, Raipur Chhattisgarh)

Abstract

Artificial Intelligence (AI) is transforming industries worldwide, and management institutions are no exception. Integrating AI into management education offers several strategic advantages, from enhancing student engagement and operational efficiency to empowering data-driven decision-making. AI will ultimately prove to be cheaper, more efficient, and potentially more impartial in its actions than human beings. In the modern world, where technological advancements continuously reshape industries, Artificial Intelligence (AI) stands as a game-changer for management institutions. AI's transformative potential extends beyond businesses and governments, with management education being one of the prime areas set to experience revolutionary growth. Integrating AI into management institutions offers numerous benefits, from improving operational efficiency to enhancing learning experiences and fostering innovative research. Here are several ways AI can contribute to the growth of management institutions:

AI-Powered Learning and Curriculum Design

The core of any management institution is its curriculum, which shapes future business leaders. AI can revolutionize how curricula are designed and delivered. Using AI algorithms, institutions can analyze massive data sets from job markets, industry trends, and student performance to tailor course content that is aligned with real-world needs. This helps ensure that students are equipped with relevant, up-to-date knowledge.

Additionally, AI can create personalized learning experiences. AI-powered platforms can assess students' strengths, weaknesses, learning styles, and progress, creating individualized learning paths. This personalization enhances the efficiency of the learning process, allowing students to grasp complex management concepts more effectively. Instructors, in turn, can utilize AI-generated insights to adapt their teaching strategies, ensuring that no student falls behind.

Personalized Learning Experiences

- AI-driven learning platforms can tailor coursework, study materials, and assignments to match each student's learning style and pace. By analyzing a student's progress and identifying their strengths and weaknesses, AI enables a more customized and engaging educational experience.
- Adaptive learning algorithms allow students to focus on areas needing improvement, fostering a more productive learning environment and leading to better academic performance.

AI-Enhanced Admissions and Student Selection

The admission process for management institutions is traditionally a rigorous procedure, involving extensive review of applications, interviews, and assessments. AI can streamline and improve this process by analyzing applicant data holistically, identifying candidates with high potential, and even predicting their success in management programs.

Machine learning algorithms can assess past academic performance, extracurricular activities, leadership qualities, and even psychological attributes like grit and resilience. By using AI, institutions can reduce human biases and select candidates based on data-driven insights, leading to a more diverse, high-quality student body.

AI Chatboats can further enhance the admission process by engaging with prospective students, answering their questions in real-time, and providing personalized guidance throughout the application process. This helps attract top talent globally, giving institutions a competitive edge

Operational Efficiency through AI Automation

- AI can significantly improve the operational efficiency of management institutions by automating administrative tasks. From scheduling classes, managing attendance, grading assignments, to handling payrolls and procurement, AI-powered automation tools can streamline these functions, reducing human error and freeing up valuable time for faculty and staff.
- For instance, Chatboats can handle routine inquiries from students and faculty, reducing the burden on administrative teams. Predictive analytics can be applied to facilities management, ensuring that resources like classrooms, libraries, and labs are optimally used. This not only leads to cost savings but also enhances the overall operational workflow of the institution.
- AI-powered tools can automate administrative tasks like admission processing, scheduling, grading, and handling routine

inquiries, freeing up faculty and staff to focus on more complex tasks.

- Predictive analytics help management institutions forecast enrollment trends, allocate resources effectively, and optimize campus operations, leading to cost savings and improved operational efficiency.

Fostering Innovation in Research and Data Analysis

- Management research is integral to advancing business practices and policies. AI can support research activities by analyzing large datasets, identifying trends, and generating insights that would be difficult for humans to uncover. AI tools can assist in literature reviews, automating the process of scanning vast amounts of academic articles to find relevant material.

- Natural Language Processing (NLP) tools can summarize complex research papers, making it easier for students and researchers to stay updated with the latest developments. Moreover, AI-driven data analytics platforms can support empirical research by processing vast amounts of business and financial data, allowing researchers to develop models that predict business outcomes or assess economic trends with greater accuracy.

- AI-powered data analytics provide faculty and students with valuable insights by quickly processing and analyzing large volumes of data, essential for research and case studies. This enables faculty to produce research that is current, data-driven, and relevant to industry needs.
- With advanced analytics, management institutions can track and measure student success, identifying trends and areas that need improvement to maintain high standards in education.

AI in Leadership Development and Simulations

- Management institutions often focus on developing leadership and decision-making skills. AI can be used to create highly realistic simulations that allow students to practice these skills in a controlled environment. AI-based simulators can model complex business scenarios, where students are required to make decisions and receive real-time feedback based on their choices.
- These simulations can include elements of risk management, strategy development, crisis response, and more, giving students hands-on experience in tackling real-world challenges. AI-driven gamification can also help foster team-building and collaborative learning, crucial for developing effective management leaders.

Data-Driven Career Support

- AI is revolutionizing career support services as well. Management institutions can use AI tools to match students with internships, job opportunities, and projects that align with their skills and aspirations. AI-powered platforms can analyze market demand and student competencies to offer personalized career advice, helping students navigate their career paths more effectively.

- Additionally, AI can assist in preparing students for interviews by analyzing their performance during mock interviews. AI tools can provide feedback on body language, tone, and the content of answers, offering detailed suggestions for improvement. This helps students gain confidence and improves their chances of securing coveted roles in top companies.

- AI can play a significant role in helping management students find relevant internships, job placements, and career development resources. Intelligent recommendation systems can match students with job openings that align with their skills, preferences, and career aspirations.
- Additionally, AI tools that analyze market trends and skill demands can guide curriculum updates, ensuring that students acquire relevant and in-demand skills for the job market.

Ethical Considerations and the Human-AI Balance

- While the potential of AI in management institutions is immense, it is crucial to strike a balance between AI tools and human intervention. Ethical considerations, such as data privacy and biases in AI algorithms, must be addressed to ensure that AI is used responsibly. Management institutions have a critical role in fostering an understanding of ethical AI use among future business leaders.
- Moreover, while AI can automate and augment many tasks, the human touch remains indispensable in education. Faculty members still play a vital role in mentoring students, fostering critical thinking, and cultivating a strong ethical foundation. AI should be seen as an enabler rather than a replacement for human expertise.

Improved Student Support Systems

- AI Chatbots and virtual assistants can support students with around-the-clock guidance on queries related to courses, admissions, deadlines, and campus resources.
- AI can also be used to monitor student mental health by analyzing patterns in engagement, coursework, and social interactions, allowing for timely intervention when students

need support.

Enhanced Faculty Productivity and Development

- By automating routine tasks, AI enables faculty to focus on delivering quality education, research, and mentoring. AI-based tools can assist instructors in creating content, evaluating assignments, and tracking student progress more efficiently.
- Additionally, faculty development programs can leverage AI-driven insights to identify skill gaps and create tailored training, ensuring educators are equipped to meet evolving industry standards.

Global and Virtual Learning Opportunities

- AI enables management institutions to offer virtual courses and expand their reach to a global audience. With AI-powered language translation and interactive simulations, institutions can provide high-quality management education to students worldwide.

- Virtual classrooms, powered by AI, enable students to collaborate and learn from industry leaders and peers across the globe, broadening their perspectives and enhancing the educational experience.

Conclusion

The integration of AI into management institutions offers unprecedented opportunities for growth. From optimizing operational efficiency and enhancing curriculum design to revolutionizing research and career support, AI is poised to redefine the way management education is delivered. As management institutions embrace AI, they will not only improve the quality of education but also prepare future leaders to navigate the increasingly complex and technology-driven business world.

By harnessing the power of AI, management institutions can stay ahead of the curve, ensuring that their students and faculty thrive in a rapidly evolving global landscape.

AI holds immense potential to drive the growth and development of management institutions, making them more adaptive, efficient, and innovative. By embracing AI, management schools can create more personalized and effective learning experiences, improve operational efficiency, and strengthen industry relevance—ensuring that they prepare students with the skills needed to thrive in a rapidly changing business landscape. For management institutions, investing in AI is not just a technological upgrade; it is a strategic move to stay competitive and relevant in an increasingly digital world.

References:

1.Acikkar, M., & Akay, M. F. (2009). Support vector machines for predicting the admission decision of a candidate to the School of Physical Education and Sports at Cukurova University. *Expert Systems with Applications, 36*(3 PART 2), 7228–7233. https://doi.org/10.1016/j.eswa.2008.09.007.
2.Adamson, D., Dyke, G., Jang, H., & Rosé, C. P. (2014). Towards an agile approach to adapting dynamic collaboration support to student needs. *International Journal of Artificial Intelligence in Education, 24*(1), 92–124. https://doi.org/10.1007/s40593-013-0012-6.
3.Brunton, J., & Thomas, J. (2012). Information management in systematic reviews. In D. Gough, S. Oliver, & J. Thomas (Eds.), *An introduction to systematic reviews,* (pp. 83–106). London:

SAGE.

4.Prediction Machines: The Simple Economics of Artificial Intelligence

5.Harvard Business Review Press, Cambridge, MA (2018)

6.https://www.forbes.com/sites/tomdavenport/2019/10/10/managing-support-knowledge-with-ai-talla-helps-toast/#4d88ade77267

7.https://doi.org/10.1287/stsc.2019.0099

8.https://www.cbinsights.com/research/ai-trends-2019/

9.https://twimlai.com/twiml-talk-217-trends-in-reinforcement-learning-with-simon-osindero/

"Artificial Intelligence and the Transformation of Indian Education: Exploring Opportunities and Overcoming Challenges"

Mr. Aaradhya Sharma
(Pursuing B. Tech. in Aero Space, VIT, Bhopal)
Dr. Deepali Gupta
(Assistant Professor, St. Paul Institute of Professional Studies, Indore)

Abstract

The integration of Artificial Intelligence (AI) into education has the potential to revolutionize how education is delivered and experienced in India. This paper examines the role of AI in transforming the Indian education landscape, focusing on the opportunities and challenges it presents. Through a comprehensive literature review and analysis of data from various sources, this research highlights the significant opportunities AI offers, such as personalized learning, improved access to education, and enhanced administrative efficiency. However, it also addresses the challenges, including data privacy concerns, accessibility issues, changes in teacher-student dynamics, and equitable AI deployment.

Keywords: Educational revolution, Digitalization, Self-learning, Technological infrastructure, Connectivity

Introduction

Artificial Intelligence: Meaning and Concept

The origins of Artificial Intelligence (AI) can be traced back to the 1950s, when Alan Turing, widely regarded as the father of AI, developed the concept of the 'Turing Machine,' which was capable of simulating human-like intelligence. John McCarthy later coined the term "AI" in 1956, defining it as "the science and engineering of creating intelligent machines" (Russel & Norvig, 2010). According to McCarthy, every aspect of learning and intelligence could theoretically be defined so precisely that a machine could replicate it.

The Indian education landscape is on the brink of a transformative revolution, driven by the rapid integration of AI. As the world's second-most populous country with a diverse and expansive education system, India faces unique challenges and unprecedented opportunities in applying AI to education. AI has the potential to significantly impact how knowledge is disseminated, learning is personalized, and educational outcomes are achieved across the nation.

Recent years have seen a significant transformation in pedagogy, driven by advancements in information and communication technology (ICT) (Sinha & Bagarukayo, 2019; Tijani, Obielodan, & Akingbemisilu, 2020). Technology has profoundly impacted educational experiences, enabling students to engage in blended learning that combines traditional classroom settings with online learning, thanks to intelligent tutoring systems and AI capabilities (Chen, MdYunus, Ali, & Bakar, 2008; Pedro, Subosa, Rivas, & Valverde, 2019). This emerging educational ecosystem reflects the changing needs of modern education.

This paper delves into AI's multifaceted role in shaping the Indian education landscape, exploring emerging opportunities and potential challenges. From improving access to quality education to enhancing administrative efficiency, AI applications in education are wide-ranging, benefiting both students and educators. However, it is equally important to address challenges such as privacy issues, equity concerns, and human-AI collaboration.

Education aims to shape individuals capable of driving future growth, ensuring the prosperity of communities and nations (King, 2011).

Objectives

1. Gain insights into how Artificial Intelligence is reshaping the education landscape in India.
2. Explore the opportunities and challenges of implementing Artificial Intelligence in the Indian education sector.

Literature Review

Artificial Intelligence, as defined by Huang, Rust, & Maksimovic (2019), includes computer programs and technologies designed to replicate human cognitive processes. AI systems can be classified into two main categories: mechanically intelligent systems, which excel at repetitive tasks, and thinking intelligent systems, capable of self-learning from data and adapting their performance. These systems acquire intelligence by assimilating diverse data types, such as text, audio, or video, using computational techniques like machine learning and deep learning.

Machine Learning (ML), as described by Mitchell (2017), involves algorithms that enable computers to improve autonomously through experience. ML mimics human learning by identifying and assimilating real-world knowledge to enhance performance. In AI, ML is a prevalent technique, particularly for applications like recommendation systems, autonomous vehicle control, image recognition, computer vision, and natural language processing.

Research Methodology

This research relies on secondary data sources, including books, scholarly articles, and comprehensive databases. These sources were selected based on predefined criteria to ensure data relevance and reliability. This approach establishes a robust foundation for research, relying on well-established and respected information repositories. Using secondary data from reputable sources enhances the credibility of the research findings and supports the academic rigor of this study.

Discussion

The role of AI in transforming the Indian education landscape is multifaceted, with the potential to revolutionize the sector. Key aspects include:

1. Personalized Learning: AI enables personalized learning experiences by analyzing students' strengths and weaknesses, allowing tailored content delivery and customized assessment.

2. Improved Access: AI can bridge educational gaps by providing access to quality education in remote or underserved areas. Virtual classrooms and AI-powered online learning platforms offer opportunities for students lacking traditional educational access.

3. Enhanced Administrative Efficiency: AI can streamline administrative tasks like enrolment, scheduling, and resource allocation, reducing administrative overhead and improving efficiency.

4. Data-Driven Decision Making: AI can analyze large educational data volumes, providing insights to educators and policymakers for curriculum development, student assessment, and policy formulation.

5. Teacher Support: AI can assist teachers by automating grading and providing lesson planning resources, allowing educators to focus more on teaching and mentoring students.

6. Language and Accessibility: AI-powered translation and speech recognition tools enhance education accessibility for students speaking different languages or with disabilities.

7. 24/7 Learning Support: AI-driven chatboats and virtual tutors provide continuous support and quick answers to students' queries, enabling learning anytime, anywhere.

8. Reducing Educational Disparities: AI can help reduce educational disparities by providing tailored support to disadvantaged students and identifying at-risk students needing extra assistance.

However, AI implementation in education also presents challenges, including data privacy concerns, digital divide, ethical use, teacher training needs, infrastructure issues, and ensuring cost and equity. Balancing these opportunities and challenges is crucial for harnessing AI's full potential in transforming Indian education.

Challenges

1. Data Privacy: Protecting student data and adhering to data privacy regulations is a significant concern.

2. Digital Divide: Ensuring equal access to technology for all students is a challenge, as not all students have access to the necessary tools.

3. Ethical Use: Preventing biases, discrimination, and misuse of AI in education is crucial for ethical AI implementation.

4. Teacher Training: Training teachers to effectively integrate AI tools into teaching is essential.

5. Infrastructure and Connectivity: Inadequate infrastructure and connectivity in many parts of India hinder effective AI implementation, especially in rural areas.

6. Cost and Equity: High implementation costs may create disparities in educational quality, making equitable access to AI-based education challenging.

Suggestions for Enhancements in Education Integrated with AI

1. **Advancing Technological Infrastructure**: Improve internet connectivity and provide access to technology devices in educational institutions and remote regions. Government initiatives should focus on expanding broadband infrastructure and providing affordable devices.

2. **Adapting Content to Local Languages**: Create educational content in regional languages to cater to India's diverse population, enhancing comprehension and engagement.

3. **Enhancing Educator Training and Development**: Implement training programs to equip educators with skills for integrating AI tools into teaching and provide avenues for professional development.

4. **Forging Partnerships with Industry**: Collaborate with technology companies to develop innovative AI-based learning solutions tailored to Indian learners and curricula.

5. **Ensuring Data Privacy and Ethical Practices**: Establish guidelines and regulations for data privacy and security in AI-based learning platforms, ensuring transparency and ethical handling of student data.

6. **Strengthening Academic-Industry Collaborations**: Promote partnerships between educational institutions and AI technology companies to develop and implement AI-based learning solutions.

7. **Ongoing Assessment and Enhancement**: Regularly assess AI-based learning platforms' effectiveness through research studies and user feedback, refining AI algorithms to better serve Indian learners.

8. **Promoting Public Awareness and Engagement**: Educate students, parents, and educators about AI's benefits and responsible use in education through awareness campaigns.

Implementing these recommendations can optimize AI-based

learning in India, ensuring equitable access to quality education and leveraging AI technologies to meet the diverse needs of learners.

Conclusion

AI is a transformative innovation in educational technology, offering numerous opportunities for learners and educators. It provides a wealth of content and instructional resources, enhancing learning and teaching processes while reducing manual efforts. The ongoing development of AI-based applications is revolutionizing the Indian education system, introducing new learning methods.

However, challenges such as inadequate infrastructure, teacher proficiency gaps, and limited financial resources impede AI adoption in India. Overcoming these challenges requires systematic AI deployment and comprehensive stakeholder awareness of AI's benefits and limitations. Equipping educators with technical skills and improving infrastructure are crucial for effectively integrating AI into the education sector.

References

1. Gupta, R., & Garg, N. (2021). Opportunities and Challenges of Artificial Intelligence in Education System of India. In M. Tomar et al. (Eds.), Proceedings of the 2nd International Conference on Artificial Intelligence and Sustainable Technologies (pp. 150-159). Springer.
2. Kumar, S., & Garg, R. (2019). Artificial Intelligence in Indian Education System: Opportunities and Challenges. In M. Tomar et al. (Eds.), Proceedings of the 1st International Conference on Artificial Intelligence and Cognitive Computing (pp. 181-189). Springer.
3. Luckin, R. (2018). The future for AI in education. Nature, 557(7705), 169-171.
4. Pai, G. (2019). Artificial Intelligence in Education in India: Exploring the Opportunities and Challenges. In D. Tripathi et al.

(Eds.), Recent Trends in Communication, Computing, and Electronics (pp. 489-500). Springer.

5. Sethi, I. K., & Dhiman, R. (2022). Artificial Intelligence in Higher Education: Challenges and Opportunities in India. In B. Sahoo et al. (Eds.), Emerging Technologies in Computer Engineering: Microservices in Big Data Analytics (pp. 27-36). Springer.

6. Sinha, S., & Bagarukayo, E. (2019). Flipped classroom for the enhancement of student learning experience and satisfaction in higher education. Journal of Computers in Education, 6(1), 1-22.

7. Tijani, R. G., Obielodan, A. R., & Akingbemisilu, A. A. (2020). A Systematic Review of Educational Technology in Nigeria: Adoption, Implementation, and Implications. International Journal of Education and Development using Information and Communication Technology, 16(1), 52-69.

8. Turing, A. M. (1950). Computing Machinery and Intelligence. Mind, 59(236), 433-460.

9. United Nations Educational, Scientific and Cultural Organization. (2022). Artificial Intelligence in Education: Challenges and Opportunities for Sustainable Development. UNESCO Publishing.

CHAPTER VIII

"From Traditional to Digital: How Artificial Intelligence transforms Commerce and Management"

Mrs. Nidhi Agrawal
(PhD. Scholar, DAVV Indore)

Prof. (Dr.) Unmekha Tare
(Dean Academics, St. Paul Institute of Professional and Management Studies, Indore)

Abstract

Artificial Intelligence has gained significantly attention in recent years, leading to profound changes across various fields. AI's capacity to analysis historical data, evaluate current conditions and forecast future trends for reshaping industry. This chapter explores the sustainable impact of AI on commerce and management, including its application Neo Banking, Fintech which caters on personalized financial services and fraud detection, in supply Chain Management AI enhances inventory control and logistics, Human Resource Management where AI scrutinized application and helps in recruitments. Furthermore, AI optimize the process and drive innovation in Strategic Decision Making and Operational Efficiency also. This Chapter also addresses the benefits and challenges associated with AI into these fields, considering ethical concerns, technological constraints and possible disruptions applicable to different fields.

Key words: Artificial Intelligence, Banking, commerce, Financial Services, Fintech, Management, Block Chain technology.

Introduction:

An ease to get everything in seconds, is the key demand of the market today. Whether its commerce, banking or management, innovation is what the industry demands, and latest is AI. Finance or banking has been always a fertile ground for technological innovation as the need is to manage vast amount of data ensure the security and also to maintain customer service. AI has reshaped finance, accuracy and customer satisfaction. From Automated trading system to AI driven customer service Chatbots, where all the questions are answered in just mini seconds, then who needs a human to solve a problem, when AI has solutions to everything.

AI also become integral part of financial operations from traditional banking to internet banking to Fintech, services are same but process have changed to heap of papers to paper less banking, everything digital. Banking Industry is one of the most stable and conservative sectors of Indian economy, but when one goes globally the latest technology has to be adopted. With the increase use of AI banking gets faster, but also remember risk also gets maximum, as unlike US, UK or Europe people are not very technology friendly to adopt these trends and this gap invites the fraudulent. This chapter deals with various application of AI in commerce including financial sector, management and their transformational impact.

AI ability to analysis large database in fractions of seconds and accuracy to detect fraudulent activities in real time can reduce financial losses which is high demand of public and private bank where lot of frauds has been done by the employees itself. For ex- with the help of Ai unusual pattern of transactions can be identified and hence reducing the risk of financial crimes.

This chapter aims to explore the various application in commerce and management field where AI has made significant impact, such as banking, investment management and risk assessment and discus the challenges and ethical considerations associated with AI adaption and also, the chapter will provide insights into future trends and opportunities insisting on the continuous evolution of AI and its implications for the financial industry.

Objectives of the paper:

This Chapter, research goal is to present a thorough analysis of the artificial intelligence (AI) role plays in Commerce and Management.

The following are the precise objectives:

1. Analyze the state of AI applications in several facets of banking, such as risk reduction, Customer service, Fintech.
2. Discuss the moral issues and dangers associated with the usage of AI in commerce and management fields, such as algorithmic bias, data privacy and security, and the need for openness and explanation.
3. Examine the upcoming developments in artificial intelligence (AI)-enabled Banking, commerce and management, taking into account the internet of things (IoT), machine learning, natural language processing, Explainable AI, Blockchain technology and robotic process automation.

By attaining these research goals, this study hopes to advance knowledge of AI's place in Commerce management and offer guidance to those who work in the field and make decisions.

AI in Banking/Fintech.

Banking has become so much versatile, and the transaction volume has also increased due to online banking and through apps on mobile. Users is expected to double between 2021 and 2022 reaching over 4 billion globally.89% of consumers (including 97%

of millennial) use mobile banking, which increases the transaction volume and also crimes. Machine learning algorithms can analysis vast amounts of transaction data in real time identifying the pattern and abnormalities that may indicate fraudulent activities and thus safeguarding the customers.AI related reports are generated and system generated POP up are also there whenever the staff do the transactions, so that staff can adequately take care of the transaction and any mishappening could be avoided.

Customer Service and Personalization:

After the banking hours, if any customer had any issues then he is directed to the phone banking, where he has to dial the number and the customer care gets connected and then discuss his query. With the automation of AI, AI driven Chatbots and virtual assistants are revolutionizing customer service in banking.

According to Rust and Huang (2014), platforms like Netflix, Hotstar used these systems to see what viewer is watching, predict and suggest the next show or movie. Similarly, Kietzmann, Paschen, and Treen (2018) features that AI-powered Chatbots and virtual assistants improve customer service by providing real-time, exact response to queries and therefore enhancing operational efficiency.

These system can handle wide range of customer queries and inquiries from basic banking to complex transaction queries, providing instant solutions and reducing wait times, previously where customer use to wait for long hours to speak to customer care representative .Additionally, AI can analyses customer data to offer personalized financial advice according to their needs ,enhancing the overall customer experience.

Case Studies of AI in Financial Services:

AI-Enabled Voice-Based Payments in Rural India:

According to an article in *The Economic Times*, Kishan Pal, a farmer from Uttar Pradesh, can dial a number from his button phone and say, "Mummy ko paisee bhejna hai" (I want to send money to mother). A pre-recorded female voice responds, "Theek hai, Kripa mobile number bataye" (Please say the mobile number). Once he provides the mobile number, the money is instantly transferred to his mother in remote UP. This process is enabled by AI-based intent analysis, which automatically recognizes the farmer's voice and preferred language. This year, the Reserve Bank of India and the National Payments Corporation of India launched voice-based payments for peer-to-peer transfers in 11 languages (Economic Times, 2024).

The Indian fintech market is expected to reach US $ 150-160 billion by 2025,prime example of Indian fintech innovation is the Unified Payments Interface (UPI) launched in 2016 the National Payments Corporation of Indian (NPCI) ,UPI has transferred digital payments in India., by enabling instant inter- bank transactions through mobile phones, decreasing cash transactions immensely.

Supply Chain Management

Globalization drives businesses to enhance their supply chains, affecting market dynamics, demand, and management. Companies must adapt to stay competitive by addressing demand uncertainty, disruptions, and financial risks (Giannakis & Papadopoulos, 2016).

Traditional supply chain management (SCM) often suffers from inefficiencies due to manual processes and limited data analysis. AI, with technologies like machine learning and predictive analytics, offers a transformative solution. By analysing large data base and providing real-time insights, AI can improve decision-making, demand for casting hitch in turn leads to better inventory management, reduced stock outs and increased customer satisfaction. This has been also highlighted by Tan et al. (2020) assert that AI optimizes logistics and inventory management through predictive analytics. By analysing historical data and identifying patterns, AI systems forecast demand, manage inventory levels, and reduce costs.

Marketing and Sales

AI is changing how businesses approach marketing and sales. According to Chaffey and Ellis-Chadwick (2019), AI tools help companies understand customer behaviour, divide markets into segments, and develop targeted marketing campaigns. AI's ability to predict customer needs allows businesses to adapt their sales strategies. Additionally, Paschen et al. (2020) highlight that AI in sales automation simplifies tasks, cuts down on manual work, and boosts efficiency.

AI in Management:

1. Investment Management:
Algorithmic trading: Algorithmic trading, driven by AI, has changed the way investments are made, with the help of these Algorithm market is studied, find trading opportunities and do the trade instantly. These can respond to the market in real time, making decisions on the past data current market conditions and predictive analysis.

2. Portfolio Management:
Now portfolio can be managed using AI, by providing advanced tool for asset allocation and risk assessment. Robo-advisors which are automated platforms by AI provide personalized advice based on individual risk tolerance and financial goals. These tools help

investors to optimize their investment portfolios by distributing the asset across various investment categories example stocks, bonds, mutual funds, real estate based on a thorough analysis of risk or return.

3. Risk Management:

4. Credit Scoring

AI improves credit scoring by using new types of data, like social media activity and online behavior along with traditional methods, this help better understanding of person's creditworthiness, especially for those with little credit history or no credit history. For instance a person consistently pays their utility bills on time but has no formal credit history then AI can recognize this positive behavior and reflect in the credit score.

5. Predictive Analysis:

AI powered predictive analysis help financial institution forecast and manage risk by analysing large amounts of past data and can predict potential market downturns and assesses the impact of economic changes .This foresight allows financial institution to make more informed decisions and develop strategies to reduce risk,

One of the advantage of predictive analysis is its ability to provide early warnings about market volatility ,for ex AI can detect small changes in consumer spending or commodity prices that might indicate an upcoming market decline.

Moreover, predictive analysis can help in operational efficiency, for ex, AI can predict cash flow needs, helping bank manage their liquidity more effectively and holding cash at end of the day. It can also foresee loan defaults by analysing the borrow behaviour and economic conditions, allowing banks to take steps to minimise losses.

Decision Making and Strategy:

AI greatly influences managerial decision-making and strategic planning. According to Davenport and Ronanki (2018) AI systems provide data-driven insights that support better decision-making. By analyzing large data, AI identifies trends, correlations, and anomalies that might be missed by human analysts enhancing strategic planning and helps managers make informed decisions. Additionally, Brynjolfsson and McAfee (2017) suggest that AI augments managerial capabilities by automating routine tasks, allowing managers to focus on higher-level strategic activities.

Human Resource Management

AI is increasingly impacting HRM, AI tools simplify the hiring process by screening resumes, doing initial interviews and using predictive analysis to evaluate candidates also manages employee performance by analysing data and offering personalized development advice .Additionally, Stone et al. (2020) highlight the importance of ensuring AI in HRM is transparent and fair.

Therefor AI – powered predictive analysis enable banks and financial institutions to anticipate and manage risk, understand customer behaviour, improve efficiency and ensure regulatory compliance. By using these advance tools, institutions can make better decisions, handle uncertainties and safeguard themselves in such constant changing market.

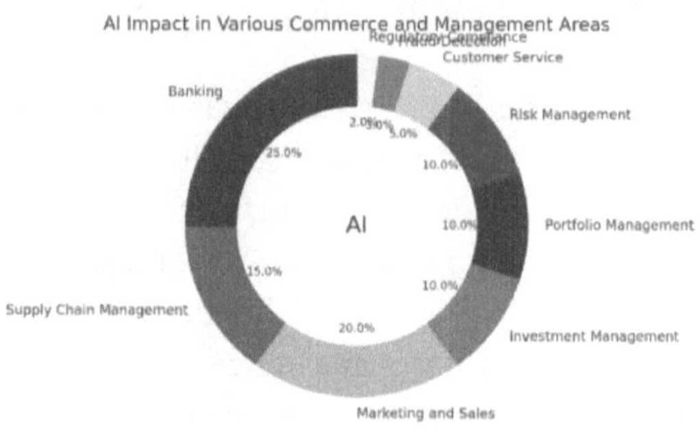

Here's the pie chart showing the impact of AI in various commerce and management areas:

Sources considered:

1. McKinsey & Company: Reports on the economic impact of AI in banking and other sectors.
2. Market Splash: Comprehensive AI banking statistics.

Challenges and Ethical Considerations:

The benefits of AI are unlimited and quite impressive, but as every coin has two sides, so it is accompanied by challenges and ethical considerations. Data Privacy and security of customer is the most challenging things which all the financial instructions are facing today in Indian economy. Today with use of AI bank fraud occur which is serious and growing problem. Customer are exposed to variety of frauds, including identity theft, account takeovers and fraudulent transactions. A report from TransUnion says fraud attempts at financial services firms increased by 149% between the end of 2020 and the end of 2021 .The Federal Trade Commission (FTC) reported that consumers will lose more than $5.8 billion to fraud in 2021, up 70% from the previous year.

Banks are using AI and Machine Learning to detect and prevent fraud. AI systems analyse corporate and retail data patterns to detect suspicious activity. But hackers are also using AI to make better plans.

Public AwarenessCampaigns: Banks and financial services companies are running campaigns to educate their customers about common frauds occur and how innocent customer are trapped with the help of case study and how to avoid them.

Transaction Failure: Banking customers are experiencing an increasing number of transaction failures through digital payments. According to data from the National Payments Corporation of India (NPCI), the volume of UPI transactions per day is more than 450 million. In May 2024 alone, there were 31 downtime instances reported from various banks, which led to the payment gateway being shut down for more than 47 hours. This has caused considerable inconvenience to users and financial losses in some cases.

For instance, on June 4th, 2024, numerous investment payments did not go through when investors wanted to capitalize on a market crash. These disruptions have raised concerns among users about the reliability of digital payment systems.

According to an article published in *The Economic Times* on June 8th, 2024, such instances have led to a decline in customer trust and satisfaction. The challenges faced by digital payment systems need to be addressed promptly to maintain the momentum of digital banking growth.

Addressing Bias in AI systems:

AI algorithms can unintentionally perpetuate biases present in historical data, leading to unfair outcomes in areas such as credit scoring and hiring practices. Financial institutions should regularly check their AI systems to find and fix these biases .Using fairness aware machine learning techniques and having diverse AI development teams are important steps to ensure AI is ethical and fair.

As globalization continues, commerce, banking are strategically planning to enhance themselves and develop their skills, significantly impacting the market, demand, data accessibility, and management. Banking need to adapt to these changes to remain competitive by mitigating demand uncertainty, avoiding disruptions, and managing financial risks. Despite its long-standing application, AI still has considerable room for development.

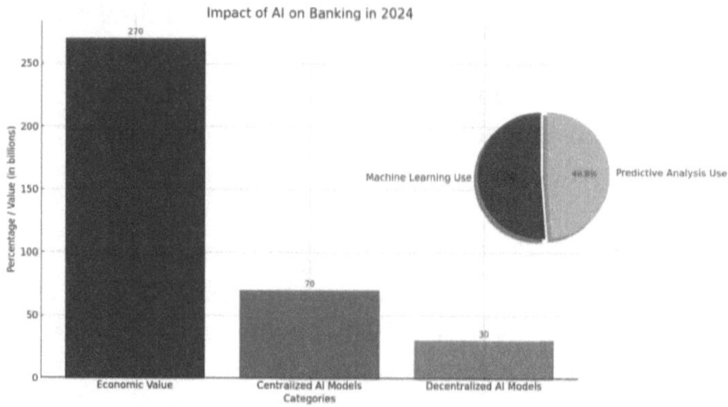

Bar Graph:

- **Economic Value:** AI could add about $270 billion annually to global banking.
- **Centralized AI Models:** 70% of banks with centralized AI models have AI in production.

- **Decentralized AI Models:** Only 30% of banks with decentralized AI models have AI in production.

Pie Chart:

- **Machine Learning Use:** 63% of investment banks use machine learning.
- **Predictive Analysis Use:** 60% of investment banks use AI for predictive analysis.

These charts highlight AI's economic value, the success of centralized AI models, and the widespread use of machine learning and predictive analysis in banking.

Sources:

- **McKinsey:** The future of AI in banking (McKinsey & Company)
- **MarketSplash:** AI Banking Statistics (MarketSplash)

Future Trends and Opportunities: According to an article in *The Economic Times*, the National Highways Authority of India (NHAI) is collaborating with IIT Delhi to leverage AI technology to enhance the availability of road signs on national highways, aiming to reduce the number of road accidents (NHAI and IIT Delhi, 2024)

The future of AI in financial services looks bright, continuous improvements in technology and data analysis. For example, combining AI with Blockchain could improve transaction security and transparency. Moreover, the development of explainable AI seeks to make AI decision-making processes clearer and more comprehensible for stakeholders. But this is just the beginning, the future of AI in India will be shaped by two major trends, greater personalization and enhanced security.

Explainable AI (XAI):

Explainable AI (XAI) is a new area focused on making AI systems' decisions clear and understandable. In financial services, XAI can increase trust by offering clear explanations for credit decisions, investment advice, and risk evaluations. This transparency is essential for meeting regulations and gaining customer confidence.

AI and Blockchain Integration:

Combining AI with Blockchain technology brings potential advantages in security and transparency. AI can enhance Blockchain by offering smart analytics and predictive capabilities, while Blockchain provides a secure and unchangeable record for AI transactions. This partnership can improve fraud detection, simplify compliance, and create new financial products and services.

Conclusion:

Artificial intelligence is revolutionizing the commerce, financial services industry, bringing new levels of innovation and efficiency. As AI advances, its use in finance will become more refined, enhancing fraud detection, customer service, investment management, and risk assessment. To fully realize AI's potential while maintaining fairness, transparency, and security, it is crucial to address the related challenges and ethical concerns. Collaboration between regulators, financial institutions, and technology developers will be key in creating robust frameworks. Additionally, ongoing education and training for stakeholders will ensure a well-informed approach to AI integration in commerce and management.

References:

1. Binns, R. (2018). Fairness in machine learning: Lessons from political philosophy. In Proceedings of the 2018 Conference on Fairness, Accountability, and Transparency (pp. 149-159).

2. Brynjolfsson, E., & McAfee, A. (2017). The Business of Artificial Intelligence: What It Can – and Cannot – Do for Your Organization. Harvard Business Review.

3. Bughin, J., Hazan, E., Ramaswamy, S., Chui, M., Allas, T., Dahlström, P. ... & Trench, M. (2017). Artificial Intelligence: The Next Digital Frontier? McKinsey Global Institute.

4. Chamorro-Premuzic, T., Akhtar, R., Winsborough, D., & Sherman, R. A. (2017). The datafication of talent: How technology is advancing the science of human potential at work. Current Opinion in Behavioral Sciences, 18, 13-16.

5. Chaffey, D., & Ellis-Chadwick, F. (2019). Digital Marketing: Strategy, Implementation, and Practice. Pearson.

6. Davenport, T. H., & Ronanki, R. (2018). Artificial Intelligence for the Real World. Harvard Business Review.

7. Floridi, L., Cowls, J., Beltrametti, M., Chatila, R., Chazerand, P., Dignum, V. ... & Schafer, B. (2018). AI4People—An ethical framework for a good AI society: Opportunities, risks, principles, and recommendations. Minds and Machines, 28, 689-707.

8. Ivanov, D., Dolgui, A., Sokolov, B., Ivanova, M., & Kalinina, O. (2019). A digital supply chain twin for managing the disruption risks and resilience in the era of Industry 4.0. Production Planning & Control, 31(2-3), 154-177.

9. Kietzmann, J., Paschen, J., & Treen, E. (2018). Artificial intelligence in advertising: Howmarketers can leverage artificial intelligence along the consumer journey. Journal of Advertising Research, 58(3), 263-267.

10. Kolbjørnsrud, V., Amico, R., & Thomas, R. J. (2016). How Artificial Intelligence Will Redefine Management. Harvard Business Review.

12. Mittelstadt, B. D., Allo, P., Taddeo, M., Wachter, S., & Floridi, L.

(2016). The ethics of algorithms: Mapping the debate. Big Data & Society, 3(2).

13. Paschen, J., Wilson, M., & Ferreira, J. J. (2020). Collaborative intelligence: How human and artificial intelligence create value along the B2B sales funnel. Business Horizons, 63(3), 403-414.

14. Rust, R. T., & Huang, M. H. (2014). The service revolution and the transformation of marketing science. Marketing Science, 33(2), 206-221.

15. Stone, D. L., Deadrick, D. L., Lukaszewski, K. M., & Johnson, K. R. (2020). The influence of technology on the future of human resource management. Human Resource Management Review, 30(3), 100713.

16. Tan, K. H., Teo, H. P., & Tay, S. J. (2020). A framework for AI governance in the supply chain. IEEE Engineering Management Review, 48(3), 151-161.

17. Dastidar, S. G. (2018). Artificial Intelligence in the Indian Banking Sector: Challenges and Opportunities. IUP Journal of Information Technology, 14(4), 7-21.

18. Gupta, A., & Gupta, A. (2019). The impact of artificial intelligence on the HR functions in the Indian IT sector. International Journal of Scientific and Technology Research, 8(9), 1047-1051.

19. Joshi, A., & Sharma, N. (2018). Artificial Intelligence in India – Hype or Reality. NASSCOM. Retrieved from NASSCOM.

20. Kapoor, B., & Kapoor, R. (2020). The Future of Artificial Intelligence in Indian Manufacturing. Journal of Information Technology Management, 31(2), 37-45.

21. Singh, A., & Malik, A. (2019). Adoption of Artificial Intelligence in E-commerce: A Case Study on Indian Context. Journal of Business and Management, 21(1), 60-69.

22. Dr Abdal Ahmed,(2023) Artificial Intelligence's Integration in Supply Chain Management: A Comprehensive Review, 13(3):1512-1527.

CHAPTER IX

"The Role of Artificial Intelligence in Modern Commerce: Innovations, Challenges, and Future Prospects"

Dr. Payal Jain
(Assistant Professor-Graduate School of Business, Indore)

Introduction

Artificial Intelligence (AI) has driven a transformative shift in commerce, evolving from traditional retail methods to sophisticated digital platforms. Initially used for basic automation tasks, AI has progressed significantly with advancements in computing and data analytics, becoming a crucial element in contemporary business practices. Today, AI is embedded in various facets of commerce, enhancing operational efficiency, customer engagement, and decision-making.

AI applications are diverse: predictive analytics forecast market trends, dynamic pricing strategies maintain competitiveness, and Chatbots provide personalized customer service. Recommendation engines further enrich user experiences by offering tailored suggestions based on detailed behavioral analysis. These advancements streamline processes and enable businesses to adapt to market changes with remarkable precision.

However, the adoption of AI brings substantial challenges. Ethical issues, such as algorithmic bias and data privacy, are significant concerns. Additionally, scaling AI solutions remains a challenge, with unequal access and expertise creating global disparities. Addressing these issues is essential to fully harness AI's capabilities.

This research investigates AI's multifaceted impact on modern commerce, analyzing innovations, challenges, and future directions. By tackling ethical concerns, improving scalability, and promoting inclusive access, businesses can leverage AI to build a more resilient and competitive future in global trade.

Purpose and Scope

This chapter aims to provide a thorough overview of AI's role in transforming the commercial landscape. We will explore key AI innovations, compare modern AI-driven practices with traditional methods, and examine the future of commerce influenced by AI advancements. By reviewing current literature, trends, and case studies, this chapter seeks to offer valuable insights for businesses, researchers, and policymakers.

Literature Review

S.Shanmugapriya, Pavithra Subramani (2024) Artificial Intelligence (AI) is pivotal in transforming the e-commerce landscape, offering substantial advantages across various dimensions of online commerce. Key roles of AI include: Personalization: AI algorithms enhance the shopping experience by analyzing customer data—such as browsing history, purchasing behavior, and preferences—to deliver personalized product recommendations and customized shopping journeys. This capability significantly boosts customer engagement and conversion rates. Customer Service: AI-powered Chatbots and virtual assistants provide round-the-clock support, efficiently handling customer inquiries and improving service availability. The review underscores how AI not only augments operational efficiency but also plays a critical role in shaping the future trajectory of e-commerce by optimizing customer interactions and driving business growth.

Dr.N.S. Lissy, Dr. L.V.R. Manoj Kumar, Dr.S. Umamaheswari (2024) this literature review has detailed the remarkable growth of the e-commerce sector, where online shopping has become increasingly central to consumer behavior. In this evolving landscape, Artificial Intelligence (AI) has emerged as a transformative force, offering innovative solutions to streamline operations, personalize customer experiences, and drive efficiency. The review provides an in-depth examination of AI's role in the e-commerce domain, covering its applications, benefits, challenges, and future trends. By systematically analyzing existing literature and case studies, the review offers valuable insights for businesses aiming to harness AI technology. These insights are crucial for maintaining competitiveness and addressing the shifting demands of consumers in the dynamic e-commerce environment.

Dr.Anil kumar Kashyap1 , Ity Sahu2 , Dr. Ajay kumar (2022) Artificial Intelligence (AI) has gained significant momentum and, despite being in its early stages, is increasingly transforming business operations across various sectors. The potential of AI to enhance e-commerce efficiency and effectiveness is evident, though its application is currently limited to major players due to complexity and high infrastructure costs. Additionally, user awareness of AI-driven e-commerce transactions remains low, leading to a scarcity of empirical studies on this topic.

This review systematically examined the literature on AI, focusing on its application within e-commerce. It highlights the fragmented nature of existing research, particularly in retail, and provides a comprehensive overview of AI subsets relevant to e-commerce, such as robotics for task automation. The study aims to assist future researchers by clarifying the functionalities of different AI technologies and their suitability for various e-commerce applications.

Richard Fedorko, Štefan Kráľ, Radovan Bačík (2021) this literature review has explored the intersection of e-commerce and artificial intelligence (AI), highlighting their fundamental concepts and the advantages they offer. The review underscores the importance of AI in e-commerce by synthesizing existing research and studies on the subject. It provides a comprehensive evaluation of AI's current role and potential future applications within the e-commerce sector. By examining the multidisciplinary impact of AI, this review offers insights into how investments can be better managed and priorities can be set for advancing e-business practices. The findings emphasize the critical role of AI in enhancing the effectiveness and efficiency of e-commerce operations.

This literature review has examined the impact of information and communication technologies (icts) on e-commerce, emphasizing the significance of investments in human capital and the strategic integration of digital solutions. The retail sector, in particular, illustrates the pronounced effects of digital transformation, where technologies such as websites increasingly complement or replace traditional physical commerce.

Ms J. Prabha, Dr. MGR (2021) This literature review has illuminated the impact of artificial intelligence (AI) on various facets of e-commerce, highlighting key findings from the analysis. The data reveals diverse usage patterns among respondents: 37.5% have engaged with e-commerce platforms for 1 to 5 years, 16.7% for more than 5 years, and 45.8% for less than one year. In terms of industry representation, 30.3% of respondents are involved in diverse domains, 12.7% in travel and tourism, and 50% in banking. The analysis further indicates varying perceptions of e-commerce effectiveness: 45.8% of respondents rated their experience as good, 12.5% as not good, and 41.7% as very good. These insights underscore the role of AI in significantly enhancing user experience on e-commerce websites, suggesting that AI-driven advancements contribute to improved customer satisfaction and engagement.

Neha Soni A, Enakshi Khular Sharma (2020) An analysis of the top 200 AI start-ups reveals the profound influence of advanced research and innovation on the global market. The findings indicate a strong and growing appetite for AI, with investment in the technology showing an upward trend over the past six years and expected to continue in the foreseeable future. The review also highlights key industries poised for significant opportunities in AI, including business intelligence, healthcare, core AI, cyber security, and marketing & sales. Notable advantages of AI-driven automation, cognitive technologies, and data analysis include increased productivity, enhanced time and cost efficiency, reduction in human error, accelerated decision-making, improved customer preference prediction, and maximized sales.

However, the review also identifies several challenges associated with AI. The technology is currently concentrated in a few regions, leading to an "AI divide" that may exacerbate social, economic, and cultural inequalities. Additionally, the reliance on software in AI introduces vulnerabilities, and despite advances, deep learning algorithms can still produce unreliable results. Challenges such as trust, ethics, bias, and a shortage of AI talent also need to be addressed to ensure the successful commercial application of AI technologies.

Historical Context of AI in Commerce

Evolution

AI's integration into commerce has advanced significantly over recent decades. Initially focused on simple automation and data analysis, early applications included expert systems for inventory and customer service. The 1980s and 1990s introduced more advanced techniques like decision trees and basic neural networks. The 2000s saw the rise of machine learning and big data, which enabled more complex decision-making and analytics. Notable milestones include Amazon's recommendation engine and advancements in natural language processing by Google. Recent developments in deep learning and AI platforms have further revolutionized commerce, enhancing predictive capabilities, pricing models, and customer personalization.

Key Milestones

Significant milestones in AI's evolution in commerce include the creation of recommendation algorithms, natural language processing tools, and autonomous systems. For example, Amazon's recommendation engine, launched in the early 2000s, represented a major advancement by personalizing user experiences based on individual browsing and purchase histories.

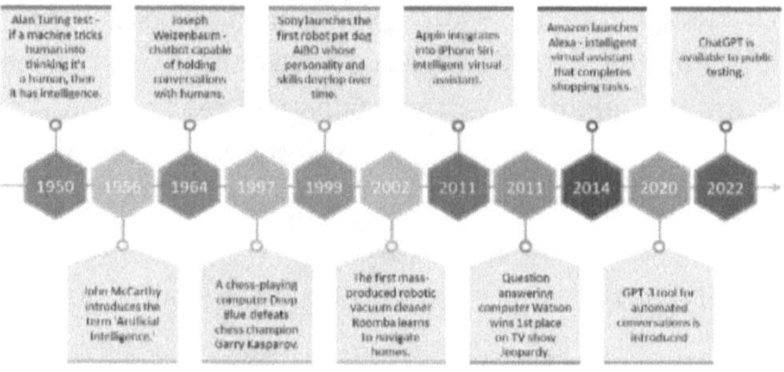

Source: https://www.infodiagram.com/slides/ ai-development-timeline/

Current Trends and Innovations

AI Technologies

AI is significantly reshaping commerce by improving efficiency and personalizing customer interactions. Machine learning algorithms process extensive data to forecast consumer behavior, optimize inventory, and streamline supply chains. AI-driven chatboats and virtual assistants offer real-time support and personalized recommendations. Marketing strategies benefit from AI tools that analyze user data to craft targeted campaigns, boosting engagement and conversions. Innovations like generative AI enhance content creation, including product descriptions and advertising materials. Additionally, AI-powered fraud detection systems enhance security by identifying and addressing fraudulent activities in real-time. The continuous advancement of AI technology promises further innovations, driving growth and improving the shopping experience.

Challenges and Criticisms

Implementing AI in business presents several challenges, including:

1. **Data Quality Issues**: The effectiveness of AI tools relies on high-quality data. Inaccurate or irrelevant data can disrupt AI applications, highlighting the need for clean, relevant, and accessible data.
2. **Protecting Data Privacy and Security**: With increased data dependency, safeguarding sensitive information and protecting user privacy from breaches is crucial.
3. **Shortage of Skilled Professionals**: AI implementation requires a skilled workforce, including data scientists and machine learning experts. The current talent shortage poses a significant challenge.
4. **Cost of AI Implementation**: Building or upgrading AI infrastructure can be expensive, particularly for small and medium-

sized businesses, potentially deterring many organizations.

5. Challenges in AI Understanding: Resistance to AI adoption often arises from stakeholders and employees who may not fully understand AI's potential or fear job displacement.

6. Compliance with Regulations: As AI solutions become more prevalent, they face stricter regulations, particularly in highly regulated sectors like healthcare and finance.

Comparison of Modern (AI Era) and Traditional Commerce

Operational Differences

Automation and Efficiency: AI enhances operational efficiency by automating repetitive tasks and optimizing workflows. In contrast, traditional commerce relies on manual processes that are time-consuming and prone to errors. AI-driven systems can process transactions, manage inventory, and analyze customer data more rapidly and accurately.

Customer Experience: AI improves customer experience through personalization and instant support. Traditional methods often involve generic interactions and slower response times. AI tools like personalized recommendation engines and real-time chatbots offer tailored experiences that enhance customer satisfaction.

Economic Impact

Cost vs. Benefit: Adopting AI in commerce can be costly, but the return on investment (ROI) is often substantial. AI-driven systems can reduce operational costs, increase revenue through improved sales strategies, and enhance customer retention. Comparative analysis shows that businesses investing in AI see significant long-term benefits despite the initial expense.

Market Trends: AI influences market dynamics by enabling businesses to respond quickly to market changes and consumer preferences. Traditional commerce methods may lack the agility and data-driven insights provided by AI, impacting competitive positioning.

Strategic Implications

Business Models: AI is reshaping business models by enabling new revenue streams and operational efficiencies. Companies are leveraging AI to develop innovative products and services, streamline supply chains, and create data-driven strategies.

Innovation: AI fosters innovation by enabling companies to experiment with new business approaches and technologies. The integration of AI into product development and marketing strategies leads to novel solutions and competitive advantages.

Future of Commerce with AI

Emerging Trends and Technologies

Predictive Analytics: Predictive analytics, powered by AI, will play a crucial role in forecasting market trends and consumer behavior. Advanced algorithms will enable businesses to anticipate customer needs and adapt strategies accordingly.

Advanced AI Systems: Future advancements in AI technologies, such as enhanced machine learning algorithms and more sophisticated NLP models, will further transform commerce. These developments will offer deeper insights, more accurate predictions, and greater automation.

Impact on the Workforce

Job Displacement and Creation: AI's impact on the workforce will be twofold: while some jobs may be displaced by automation, new roles will emerge in AI development, maintenance, and oversight. The shift will require a workforce skilled in AI technologies and data analytics.

Skills and Training: To keep pace with AI advancements, there will be a growing need for skills in data science, machine learning, and AI ethics. Training programs and educational initiatives will be essential to prepare the workforce for these changes.

Ethical and Regulatory Considerations

Regulation: As AI continues to evolve, regulatory frameworks will need to address issues related to data privacy, algorithmic accountability, and ethical use of technology. Policymakers will play a crucial role in shaping these regulations.

Ethical Practices: Ethical considerations in AI usage include ensuring transparency, fairness, and accountability in AI systems. Ongoing debates focus on how to balance innovation with ethical practices.

Conclusion

In conclusion, AI is fundamentally reshaping the commercial landscape by enhancing operational efficiency, personalizing customer experiences, and driving strategic innovation. Its integration into commerce has evolved from basic automation to sophisticated systems capable of predictive analytics, dynamic pricing, and personalized recommendations. Despite these advancements, the path to successful AI adoption is fraught with challenges, including data quality issues, privacy concerns, a shortage of skilled talent, and high implementation costs. Traditional commerce practices are increasingly being outpaced by AI-driven methods, which offer greater agility, accuracy, and cost-effectiveness.

Looking ahead, the future of commerce with AI promises further transformation through emerging technologies and advanced systems. Predictive analytics and improved machine learning algorithms will enable businesses to anticipate market trends and adapt with greater precision. However, the transition will also necessitate addressing ethical and regulatory concerns, ensuring transparency, fairness, and accountability in AI applications. Balancing these factors while fostering a skilled workforce will be crucial for leveraging AI's full potential. By navigating these complexities, businesses can harness AI to drive growth, enhance competitive positioning, and shape a resilient and innovative future for global commerce.

Reference:

1.https://www.researchgate.net/publication/361675958_Artificial_Intelligence_in_E-commerce_A_Literature_Review
2.https://www.researchgate.net/publication/379566725_artificial_intelligence_and_e-commerce
3.A study on impact of artificial intelligence in e-commerce-https://ijcrt.org/papers/ijcrtg020005.pdf
4.A Study On Artificial Intelligence In The E-Commerce Industry-https://migrationletters.com/index.php/ml/article/view/7806
5.Artificial Intelligence in Business: From Research and Innovation to Market Deployment-https://www.sciencedirect.com/science/article/pii/S1877050920307389
6.Artificial intelligence and its applications in ecommerce - a review analysis and research agenda -https://www.jatit.org/volumes/Vol100No24/12Vol100No24.pdf

7.https://appinventiv.com/guide/artificial-intelligence-in-business/

"Ethical Challenges in Ai–Driven Management Decision Making: Addressing Bias, Transparency and Accountability"

Dr. Danish Khan
(Assistant Professor, St. Paul Institute of Professional Studies, Indore)

Dr. Anubhuti Sharma
(Associate Professor, St. Paul Institute of Professional Studies, Indore)

Abstract

The increasing reliance on Artificial Intelligence (AI) in management decision-making introduces a multitude of ethical challenges that must be meticulously addressed to ensure responsible and equitable outcomes. This paper explores the ethical considerations in AI-driven decision-making within management, focusing on key issues such as bias, transparency, and accountability. The paper begins by highlighting the significance of AI in modern management and the potential ethical pitfalls that accompany its integration. Through a review of current literature, this paper examines the prevalence of bias in AI algorithms, the challenges of achieving transparency in AI processes, and the complexities of accountability when decisions are influenced by AI systems. By analyzing recent case studies and statistics, the discussion provides insights into how these ethical concerns manifest in real-world scenarios. The paper concludes by offering suggestions for mitigating these ethical risks and calls for the development of robust frameworks that prioritize ethical considerations in AI-driven management practices.

Keywords: AI Ethics, Management Decision-Making, Bias in Algorithms, AI Transparency and Accountability.

Introduction

Artificial Intelligence (AI) has rapidly become a cornerstone in the evolution of management practices, revolutionizing decision-making processes across industries. By automating complex tasks and providing data-driven insights, AI systems offer unparalleled efficiency and accuracy, enabling organizations to make informed decisions swiftly. However, the integration of AI into management decision-making is not without ethical concerns. As AI systems increasingly influence decisions that impact employees, customers, and stakeholders, issues such as bias, transparency, and accountability come to the forefront, raising questions about the ethical implications of relying on these systems.

In recent years, the deployment of AI in decision-making has grown exponentially. According to a report by McKinsey, the adoption of AI in standard business processes has increased by 25% from 2020 to 2023, with 56% of organizations now incorporating AI in some form into their management practices **(McKinsey, 2023)**. This widespread adoption underscores the necessity of addressing the ethical challenges that accompany AI's role in decision-making. This paper aims to explore these ethical considerations, focusing on how they manifest in management and proposing strategies to mitigate potential risks.

Literature review

Bias in AI Algorithms

One of the most significant ethical challenges in AI-driven decision-making is the presence of bias in algorithms. Bias in AI can occur at various stages of the decision-making process, from data collection to algorithm design and deployment. Research has shown that AI systems can inadvertently perpetuate existing biases in data, leading to discriminatory outcomes. For instance, a study conducted by **Obermeyer et al. (2019)** revealed that an AI algorithm used in the healthcare sector exhibited racial bias, as it systematically underestimated the health needs of Black patients compared to White patients. This bias arose from the algorithm's reliance on historical data that reflected existing disparities in healthcare access and treatment.

In the context of management, biased AI algorithms can lead to unfair hiring practices, biased performance evaluations, and unequal opportunities for career advancement. A study by **Raghavan et al. (2020)** highlights the risks of AI-driven hiring tools, which can perpetuate gender and racial biases if the training data is not representative of diverse populations. This can result in the exclusion of qualified candidates based on biased criteria, thereby exacerbating existing inequalities in the workplace.

Transparency in AI Systems

Transparency is another critical ethical consideration in AI-driven decision-making. The "black box" nature of many AI systems makes it difficult for stakeholders to understand how decisions are made, raising concerns about the fairness and reliability of these decisions. Lack of transparency can undermine trust in AI systems and lead to skepticism among employees and stakeholders who are affected by AI-driven decisions.

Several scholars have emphasized the importance of transparency in AI systems. **Binns (2018)** argues that transparency is essential for ensuring accountability and enabling stakeholders to challenge or question AI-driven decisions. However, achieving transparency in AI systems is challenging due to the complexity of machine learning algorithms and the proprietary nature of many AI tools. Despite these challenges, there is a growing consensus that transparency is crucial for ethical AI deployment in management.

Accountability in AI-Driven Decision-Making

Accountability is a fundamental ethical principle that becomes increasingly complex in the context of AI-driven decision-making. When AI systems are used to make decisions, it becomes difficult to determine who is responsible for the outcomes—whether it is the developers who designed the algorithm, the managers who implemented the system, or the AI itself. This "accountability gap" raises significant ethical concerns, particularly when AI-driven decisions have negative consequences for individuals or organizations.

Wachter et al. (2020) discuss the challenges of assigning accountability in AI-driven decision-making, emphasizing the need for clear guidelines and regulations to address this issue. They argue that without proper accountability mechanisms, organizations may be reluctant to take responsibility for the outcomes of AI-driven decisions, leading to a lack of recourse for those affected by these decisions. This is particularly concerning in management, where AI-driven decisions can impact employee livelihoods, customer satisfaction, and overall organizational performance.

Discussion

Ethical Implications of AI Bias in Management

The ethical implications of AI bias in management are profound and far-reaching. When biased AI systems are used in hiring, performance evaluations, or resource allocation, they can perpetuate and even exacerbate existing inequalities within organizations. For example, if an AI system is trained on historical data that reflects gender disparities in promotions, it may continue to favor male employees over equally qualified female employees, reinforcing the glass ceiling effect.

Recent statistics highlight the prevalence of AI bias in management. A 2023 survey by the World Economic Forum found that 45% of companies using AI in HR practices reported concerns about bias in their AI tools (World Economic Forum, 2023). This statistic underscores the need for organizations to critically evaluate the data used to train AI systems and implement measures to mitigate bias. Failure to address AI bias can lead to reputational damage, legal challenges, and decreased employee morale, all of which can negatively impact organizational performance.

The Challenge of Transparency in AI-Driven Management

Transparency in AI-driven management is essential for ensuring that decisions are made fairly and equitably. However, the complexity of AI systems often makes it difficult for managers and employees to understand how decisions are made. This lack of transparency can lead to a sense of mistrust and uncertainty among employees, who may feel that AI-driven decisions are arbitrary or biased.

One of the key challenges in achieving transparency is the "black box" nature of many AI systems. These systems often operate using complex algorithms that are not easily interpretable by humans. As a result, it can be difficult for managers to explain how a particular decision was reached, leading to concerns about the fairness and accountability of AI-driven decisions.

To address this challenge, organizations must prioritize the development of transparent AI systems that allow for greater interpretability and understanding. This may involve using simpler algorithms, providing explanations for AI-driven decisions, and involving human oversight in the decision-making process. By enhancing transparency, organizations can build trust in AI systems and ensure that decisions are made in an ethical and accountable manner.

Addressing Accountability in AI-Driven Decision-Making

The issue of accountability is perhaps the most complex ethical challenge in AI-driven decision-making. When decisions are influenced by AI systems, it can be difficult to determine who is responsible for the outcomes. This lack of accountability can lead to significant ethical and legal challenges, particularly when AI-driven decisions have negative consequences.

One approach to addressing the accountability gap is to establish clear guidelines for AI use in management. This may involve defining the roles and responsibilities of managers, developers, and other stakeholders in the AI decision-making process. Additionally, organizations should consider implementing oversight mechanisms to ensure that AI-driven decisions are subject to human review and can be challenged if necessary.

Another important consideration is the need for legal and regulatory frameworks that address the unique challenges of AI-driven decision-making. Governments and regulatory bodies must work together to develop laws and regulations that hold organizations accountable for the outcomes of AI-driven decisions. This may involve creating new legal standards for AI transparency, fairness, and accountability, as well as providing mechanisms for individuals to seek redress if they are harmed by AI-driven decisions.

Suggestions and recommendations

To mitigate the ethical risks associated with AI-driven decision-making in management, organizations should consider the following recommendations:

1. Implement Bias Mitigation Strategies: Organizations should take proactive steps to identify and mitigate bias in AI systems. This may involve using diverse and representative data sets, regularly auditing AI algorithms for bias, and involving diverse teams in the development and deployment of AI systems.

2. Enhance Transparency: Organizations should prioritize transparency in AI-driven decision-making by using interpretable algorithms, providing explanations for AI-driven decisions, and involving human oversight in the decision-making process. This can help build trust in AI systems and ensure that decisions are made fairly and equitably.

3. Establish Accountability Mechanisms: Organizations should establish clear guidelines for AI use in management and implement oversight mechanisms to ensure that AI-driven decisions are subject to human review. Additionally, legal and regulatory frameworks should be developed to hold organizations accountable for the outcomes of AI-driven decisions.

4. Promote Ethical AI Practices: Organizations should promote a culture of ethical AI use by providing training and resources to employees, encouraging ethical decision-making, and fostering open dialogue about the ethical implications of AI in management.

Conclusion

As AI continues to play an increasingly prominent role in management decision-making, it is essential to address the ethical challenges that accompany its integration. Bias, transparency, and accountability are key ethical considerations that must be carefully managed to ensure that AI-driven decisions are fair, equitable, and responsible. By implementing bias mitigation strategies, enhancing transparency, establishing accountability mechanisms, and promoting ethical AI practices, organizations can mitigate the ethical risks associated with AI-driven decision-making and build trust in AI systems. As the use of AI in management continues to evolve, it is imperative that organizations remain vigilant in addressing these ethical challenges and prioritizing the responsible use of AI in decision-making.

References

1.Akinrinola, O., Okoye, C. C., Ofodile, O. C., & Ugochukwu, C. E. (2024). Navigating and reviewing ethical dilemmas in AI development: Strategies for transparency, fairness, and accountability. GSC Advanced Research and Reviews, 18(3), 050-058.

2.Binns, R. (2018). Fairness in Machine Learning: Lessons from Political Philosophy. Proceedings of the 2018 Conference on Fairness, Accountability, and Transparency. Mckinsey & Company. (2023). The State of AI in 2023. McKinsey Global Institute.

3.Li, Z. (2024). Ethical frontiers in artificial intelligence: navigating the complexities of bias, privacy, and accountability. International Journal of Engineering and Management Research, 14(3), 109-116.

4.Obermeyer, Z., Powers, B., Vogeli, C., & Mullainathan, S. (2019). Dissecting Racial Bias in an Algorithm Used to Manage the Health of Populations. Science, 366(6464), 447-453.

5.Osasona, F., Amoo, O. O., Atadoga, A., Abrahams, T. O., Farayola, O. A., & Ayinla, B. S. (2024). Reviewing the ethical implications of AI in decision making processes. International Journal of Management & Entrepreneurship Research, 6(2), 322-335.

6.Raghavan, M., Barocas, S., Kleinberg, J., & Levy, K. (2020). Mitigating Bias in Algorithmic Hiring: 7.Evaluating Claims and Practices. Proceedings of the 2020 Conference on Fairness, Accountability, and Transparency.

8.Tatineni, S. (2019). Ethical Considerations in AI and Data Science: Bias, Fairness, and Accountability. 9.International Journal of Information Technology and Management Information Systems (IJITMIS), 10(1), 11-21.

10.Wachter, S., Mittelstadt, B., & Russell, C. (2020). Why Fairness Cannot Be Automated: Bridging the Gap 11.Between EU Non-Discrimination Law and AI. Computer Law & Security Review, 36, 105365.

12.World Economic Forum. (2023). The Future of Jobs Report 2023. World Economic Forum.

CHAPTER XI

"A Study on Influence of Demographical Factors on Online Grocery Shopping – With Special Reference to Female Buyers"

Dr. Sarita Rana
(Associate Professor, Acropolis Faculty of Management and Research)

Abstract

Retailing in India is witnessing drastic changes since the time network has been accessible to all. People nowadays are switching from traditional kirana shops to modern organized retail whether it be online or offline. Today due to the wide organized retail market it has become difficult for the marketers to analyze the changing behavior of customers to ensure sustainability of the business. Many studies have been carried out to assess the shopping intentions, shopping motives and other related issues. By studying these factors in isolation is not enough, unless the demographical factors such as age, education, occupation, income etc. are the major factors which influence the buying behavior and buying intentions of the customers buying online grocery. This paper examines the influence of demographical factors towards the customer's shopping orientation, frequency of shopping, expenses towards shopping. A total of 250 questionnaires were circulated with female buyers who shop online grocery to study the influence of demographical factors on them. The survey was conducted in the Indore district of Madhya Pradesh of India.

Keyword: Online Grocery, Demographical Factors, Female Buyers

1. Introduction

Technological advancement had increased dramatically in the last 20 years. Because of this advancement, life of the consumer have become smoother and easier going nowadays. People after such advancement can now purchase anything they like by just one click on their devices instead of the physically going and purchasing. This technology has proved beneficial in the pandemic which occurred in 2020 where all people were stuck at home but the life was continuing, in order to survive people bought their essentials through online method. Because of this practice, buying behavior of consumers have changed a lot, people were left with no other option than buying grocery online. This was not only the case it has many limitation also, people who were addicted to traditional approach for such necessities faced difficulty , but the things are changing recently. The use of digital technology has led to great change in the habits of people.

Today due to the intense competition in the market, old traditional marketers are also accepting the change in the method of shopping by the consumers as to survive in the long run. Many studies have been conducted in the past to assess behavior of shoppers, shopping motives and shopping intentions and related issue but studying these factors in isolation are not much of nay use, unless demographical (personal) factors are examined. Perhaps demographical factors like age, education, occupation, marital status etc. are the major factors which influence the buying behavior of consumers other than store elements. The paper examines the influence of demographical factors on consumers shopping behavior such as frequency of shopping and monthly grocery expenses.

2. Review of Literature

Age:
It is generally assumed that with the increase in age people not like to go for online shopping as they are not familiar with the information technology, which affects their acceptance of online shopping and view is supported by Sulaiman et al (2008) younger generations use online shopping more likely as compared to older generations as the former understands the computer technology more easily.

Education:
Kim and Kim (2004) in their study indicated that more educated consumers tend to purchase grocery online and education influences the acceptance and adoption of online shopping. This study included whether education has it effects on frequency of online shopping or not.

Occupation:
This variable according to the previous studies depicts that different people with different occupation has different purchasing pattern also people with different occupation have different needs and preference regarding shopping Armstrong and kotler (2003). This study considers this variable and aim to reveal possible relations between occupation and consumers purchasing method.

Marital Status:
Hashim et al (2009) depicts that divorced consumers are more likely to shop online than the married or unmarried ones. But married consumers shop grocery online as they have dual income advantage, but generality on this subject is difficult to be suggested brown and venkatesh (2005). Apart from these findings studies relating to this topic is scarce and limited. However this subject is considered in the present study and its relationship with the consumer's frequency of shopping is examined.

Household Income

Household income has positive relationship with the online grocery shopping suggested by lohse and Spiller (2000), Mohsuwe et al (2004) suggested people with higher income tends to shop online more as compared to people with lesser income. This study helps to find out more about relationship between household income shopping habits of consumers.

3. Need of The Study

India is the fastest growing economy, rising hotspot in making their trade needs. In the past few years India has seen giants like Walmart entering its territory and has huge user base for company like Facebook, at its heart 50% growth is of women population, which is expected to drive approximately 85% of the purchase decision of the household. And with more women entering the labour force, having access to more disposable income we can't ignore the power the women have today. Talking about the power of women we can't limit just to grocery shopping nowadays specifically about India about 25.6% out of total 127 million females are forming part of working class and are actively involved in decision making, even they adding to the property by buying a car, they have changed a lot from earlier days. Women have become more informed and demanding, with the availability of abundance of products, services and increasing online channels. Their earning and spending power has increased which gives them more confidence and security. So this study focuses on the demographical factors (personal factors) influencing female consumers to purchase grocery online.

Research Methodology

The present study focuses on the impact of demographical factors on female shopping grocery items through online platforms. The population consists of the women of different occupation, household income, marital status and different age groups. The population consisted of 300 women. The Random sampling method was used to choose 50 percent of the population as sample out of which 38 responses were not filled fully.

Sources of Data: Primary Data was collected from women of different occupation, age groups, marital status and household income groups shopping grocery through electronic platforms.
Nature of Study: In the present study quantitative data was used.
Tool Used in Study: To Analyse the demographical factors impacting the women to shop grocery through online platforms a questionnaire consisting questions based on Likert scale was used.
Statistical Technique: To analyse the raw data of different factors influencing female buyers to shop grocery online ANOVA single factor has been used.

4. Objective of The Study

To study the influence of demographical factors towards online grocery shopping of female buyers.

5. Demographic Factors

In this study demographical factors (personal factors) have been analyzed like educational qualification, Occupation, marital Status, Monthly Income and Number of Working Members. Every factor has different categories from where various respondents belong. Below are some graphs which represents influence of such factors on consumer's frequency of shopping while shopping grocery online.

6.1 Educational qualification

Educational Qualification here includes categories like Uneducated, less than graduation, graduation and post-graduation.

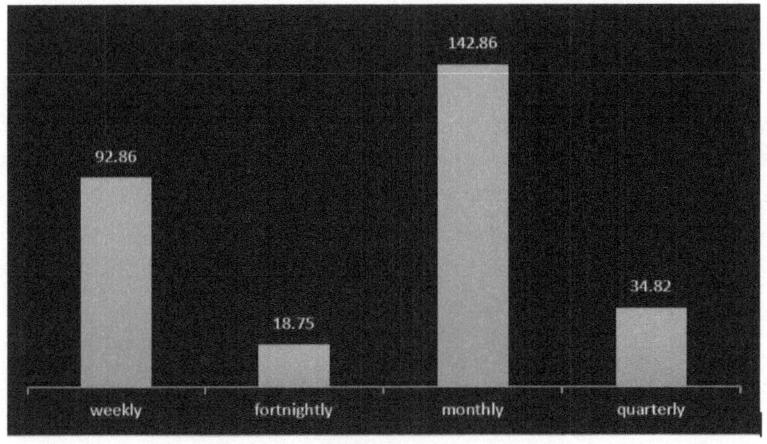

Interpretation: Above displayed graph is based on the responses of 112 female consumers of different educational background like some were uneducated, some were having qualification less than graduation, some were graduate and the others post graduate, based their educational qualification their frequency of shopping has been examined like 92% of female consumers purchased grocery weekly, 18% purchased grocery fortnightly, 142% of all purchased monthly and 34% purchased quarterly.

6.2 Marital status

Marital status here includes categories like married and unmarried.

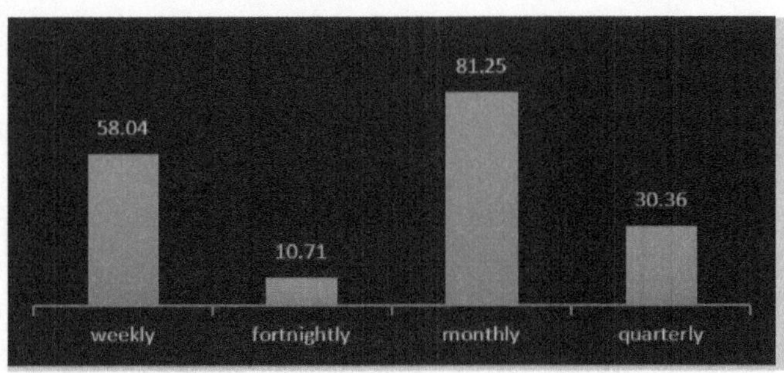

Interpretation: Above displayed graph is based on the responses of 112 female consumers of different marital status like some of them were married and some were unmarried, based on their marital status their frequency of shopping has been examined where 58% female bought online grocery weekly, 10% bought online grocery fortnightly, 815 bought online grocery monthly and 30% bought online grocery quarterly.

6.3 Monthly Income

Monthly Income here includes four categories that are upto 5000, from 5001-15000, from 15001-25000 and above 25000

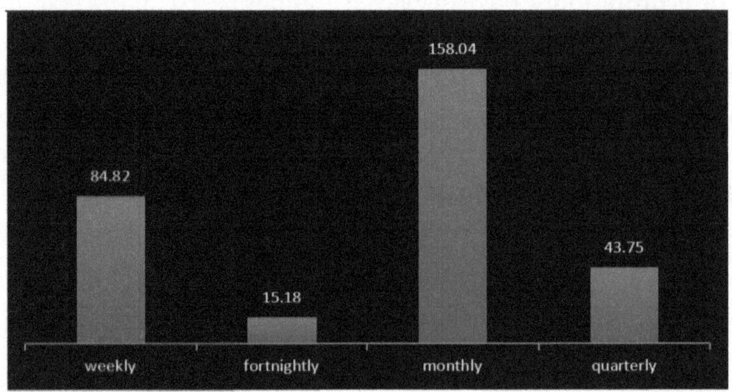

Interpretation: Above displayed graph is based on the responses of 112 female consumers of different categories belonging to monthly household income like respondents having upto 5000 of income, from 5001-15000, from 15001-25000 and above 25000, based on these categories their influence on frequency of shopping has been studied where 84% purchased online grocery weekly, 15%

purchased online grocery fortnightly, 158% of all purchased online grocery monthly and 43% purchased online grocery quarterly.

6.4 Occupation

Occupation here includes categories like student, business, service, profession and homemaker.

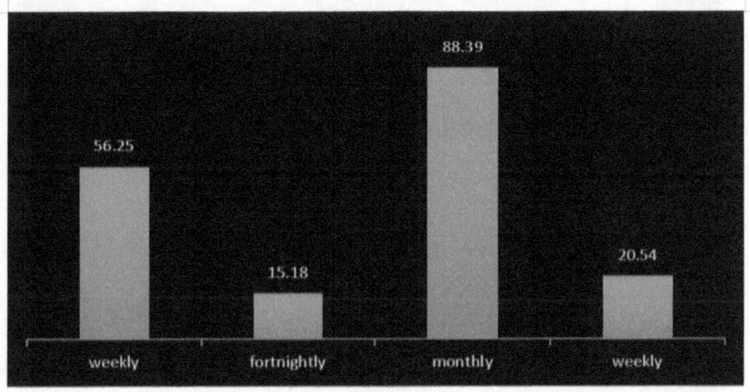

Interpretation: Above graph displayed is based on responses of 112 female consumers of different occupational categories like student, business, service, profession and homemaker and their influence on grocery shopping where 56% bought online grocery weekly, 15% bought online grocery fortnightly, 88% bought online grocery monthly and 20% bought online grocery weekly.

6.5 Number of Working Members

Number of working members here includes categories like one working member, two working members, three working members and more than three working members.

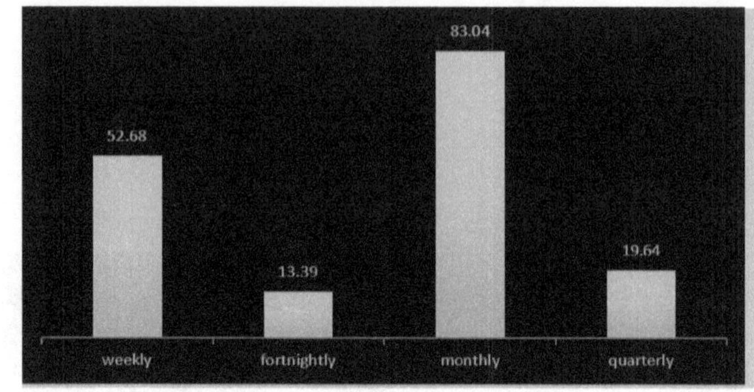

Interpretation: Above displayed graph is based on responses of 112 female consumers of different families like family having only one as their working member, family having two working members, family having three working members and family having more than three working members and their influence on grocery shopping where 52% bought online grocery weekly, 13% bought online grocery fortnightly, 83% bought online grocery monthly and 19% bought online grocery quarterly.

Hypothesis

In the present study influence of various demographical factors have been examined like educational qualification, marital status, monthly income, occupation and number of working members in the family. Questionnaire was sent to the female consumers and responses were analyzed with the help of analysis of variance test.

7.1 Educational Qualification

H0: There is no significant relationship between educational qualification and frequency of shopping of the female consumer shopping grocery online.

H1: There is a significant relationship between educational qualification and frequency of shopping of the female consumers shopping grocery online.

Table 7.1 ANOVA single factor test between educational qualification and frequency of shopping

SUMMARY TABLE				
Groups	Count	Sum	Average	Variance
weekly	35	104	2.971428571	0.734453782
fortnightly	7	21	3	0.666666667
monthly	53	160	3.018867925	0.788098694
quarterly	17	39	2.294117647	0.220588235

ANOVA TABLE					
Source of Variation	SS	df	MS	F	P-value	F crit
Between Groups	7.232313303	3	2.410771101	3.543226595	0.017057741	2.688691475
Within Groups	73.48197241	108	0.680388633			
Total	80.71428571	111				

Interpretation: From the above table it can be depicted that value of F (3.54) is greater than critical value of F (2.68), therefore Null Hypothesis is rejected leading to acceptance of alternate hypothesis for the given test.

Result: From the above test it can be concluded that alternate hypothesis is accepted which means there is a significant difference between educational qualification and the frequency of shopping of female consumers. This depicts positive relationship between two variables that is more educated people tends to shop grocery online more.

7.2 Marital Status

H0: There is no significant difference between marital status and frequency of shopping of the female consumer shopping grocery online.

H1: There is significant difference between marital status and frequency of shopping of the female consumer shopping grocery online.

Table 7.2 ANOVA single factor test between Marital Status and Frequency of Shopping

SUMMARY TABLE				
Groups	Count	Sum	Average	Variance
weekly	35	65	1.857142857	0.12605042
fortnightly	7	12	1.714285714	0.238095238
monthly	53	91	1.716981132	0.20682148
quarterly	17	34	2	0

ANOVA TABLE						
Source of Variation	SS	df	MS	F	P-value	F crit
Between Groups	1.209568733	3	0.403189578	2.644026187	0.052886	2.688691
Within Groups	16.4690027	108	0.152490766			
Total	17.67857143	111				

Interpretation: From the above table it is depicted that value of F (2.64) is lesser than the critical value of F (2.68), which means Null Hypothesis is accepted and Alternate Hypothesis is rejected for the given test.

Result: From the above test it can be inferred that acceptance of Null Hypothesis means there is no significance difference between marital status and frequency of shopping of the female consumers, that means marital status of female buyers does not impact their shopping habits while shopping grocery online.

7.3 Monthly Income

H0: There is no significant difference between Monthly Household Income and Frequency of Shopping of the female consumers shopping grocery online
H1: There is a significant difference between Monthly Household Income and frequency of Shopping of the female consumers shopping grocery online

Table 7.3 ANOVA single factor test between Monthly Household Income and Frequency of Shopping

SUMMARY TABLE				
Groups	Count	Sum	Average	Variance
weekly	35	95	2.714286	1.563025
fortnightly	7	17	2.428571	1.952381
monthly	53	177	3.339623	0.882438
quarterly	17	49	2.882353	0.860294

ANOVA TABLE						
Source of Variation	SS	df	MS	F	P-value	F crit
Between Groups	11.45564	3	3.818548	3.312246	0.022812	2.688691
Within Groups	124.5086	108	1.152858			
Total	135.9643	111				

Interpretation: From the above table it can be depicted that value of F (3.31) is greater than the critical value of F (2.68) therefore Null Hypothesis is rejected and Alternate Hypothesis is accepted for the given test.

Result: From the above test, it can be seen that alternate hypothesis is accepted which means there is a significant difference between monthly household income and frequency of shopping, it can be inferred that it has the positive relationship between the monthly household income and frequency of shoppers that is higher earning income will tends to shop more number of times.

7.4 Occupation

H0: There is no significant difference between occupation and frequency of shopping of female consumers shopping grocery online

H1: There is significance difference between occupation and frequency of shopping of female consumers shopping grocery online

<u>Table 7.4 ANOVA single factor test between Occupation and Frequency of Shopping</u>

SUMMARY TABLE				
Groups	Count	Sum	Average	Variance
weekly	35	63	1.8	1.4
fortnightly	7	17	2.428571	3.285714
monthly	53	99	1.867925	1.616836
quarterly	17	23	1.352941	0.992647

ANOVA TABLE						
Source of Variation	SS	df	MS	F	P-value	F crit
Between Groups	6.406461	3	2.135487	1.378787	0.253187	2.688691
Within Groups	167.2721	108	1.548816			
Total	173.6786	111				

Interpretation: From the above table it can be seen that value of F (1.37) is lesser than the critical value of F (2.68) therefore Null Hypothesis is accepted and Alternate Hypothesis is rejected for the given test.

Result: From the above test it can be depicted that with the acceptance of null hypothesis it can be inferred that there is no significant difference between occupation and frequency of shopping. People with different occupation tends to buy grocery with their convenience so there is no such relationship between the occupation and their frequency to buy grocery online.

7.5 Number of Working Members

H0: There is no significant difference between number of working members and frequency of shopping of female consumers shopping grocery online
H1: There is a significant difference between number of working members and frequency of shopping of female consumers shopping grocery online.

<u>Table 7.5 ANOVA single factor test between Number of Working Members and Frequency of Shopping</u>

SUMMARY TABLE				
Groups	Count	Sum	Average	Variance
weekly	35	59	1.685714	0.751261
fortnightly	7	15	2.142857	1.809524
monthly	53	93	1.754717	0.611756
quarterly	17	22	1.294118	0.345588

ANOVA TABLE						
Source of Variation	SS	df	MS	F	P-value	F crit
Between Groups	4.321767	3	1.440589	2.109874	0.103205	2.688691
Within Groups	73.74073	108	0.682785			
Total	78.0625	111				

Interpretation: From the above table it can be seen that value of F (2.10) is lesser than the critical value of F (2.68) therefore accepting the Null Hypothesis and rejecting the Alternate

Hypothesis for the given test.

Result: From the results of the above test it accepts the null hypothesis and rejects the alternate hypothesis which means there is no significant relationship between number of working members and frequency of shopping, as if the number of family members are more the expenses tends to be more but not specifically for grocery needs.

Findings and Suggestions

From the present study influence of demographical (personal factors) is examined and following interpretation have been made:

1. From table 1 it can be studied that value of F (3.54) is greater than the critical value of F (2.68) therefore rejects the null hypothesis and accepts the alternate hypothesis leading to conclusion that there exist a significant relationship between educational qualification and the respondents frequency of shopping, which depicts education affects their shopping habits more educated people have a higher percentage of adoption and acceptance of online shopping. Here mean is highest in case of monthly shopping (3.01) which means more number of educated female consumers purchase grocery once in a month.

2. From table 2 it can be depicted that value of F (2.64) is lesser than the critical value of F (2.68) which accepts the null hypothesis and rejects the alternate hypothesis which means there is no significant relationship between marital status of an individual and frequency of shopping. As grocery is needed by everyone irrespective of their marital status, being essential commodity for human survival so marital status of individual does not impact grocery shopping habits of women consumer. Also here mean (2.00) is highest in case of women shopping grocery quarterly.

3. From table 3 it can be inferred that value of F (3.31) is greater than critical value of F (2.68) which rejects the null hypothesis and accepts the alternate hypothesis that means there is a significant relationship between monthly household income of an individual and its frequency of shopping grocery online. Income of an individual decides its habits of spending, here it shows positive relationship between monthly household income and frequency of shopping which means higher the income of people more chances of them buying products online. Also here highest mean value (3.33) shows maximum number of people shops for grocery online on monthly basis as per their income availability.

4. From table 4 it can be depicted that value of F (1.37) is lesser than the critical value (2.68) which accepts the null hypothesis and rejects the alternate hypothesis with a fact that there is no significant relationship between occupation and frequency of shopping grocery online. This study depicts people with different occupation tends to buy different things at their convenience, buying habits of people are not dependent on their occupation. Also highest mean value (2.42) infers that many women consumers with different occupation tends to shop grocery online once in every fortnight.

5. From table 5 it can be studied that value of F (2.10) is lesser than the critical value (2.68) which accepts the null hypothesis and rejects the alternate hypothesis with a result that there is no significant relationship between number of working members in the family and its frequency to shop grocery online, as more number of working members leads to big family and more expenses that does not necessarily must be meant for grocery shopping, different members can have different ways of spending their income. Also here highest mean value (2.14) means more number of female consumers shop grocery through online platforms once in a fortnight.

From the above findings, following suggestions have been provided:

Education and Training

Many people of different age groups were not educated enough to use the services provided by the e-Retailers, this can solved by making them aware about the services which can be done with aggressive marketing, putting the tutorial videos on the online platform, organizing workshops and partnering with local community organizations to provide training sessions.

Customization and personalization

Not all demographic groups can have same preferences various income groups people can have various different preferences, this can be look after upon by e-retailers as they can work on their online platforms in making them more user friendly and more customizing kind of platform so that various different income group of people be able to find product of their own choice.

Delivery and Accessibility

Customers with different occupation and different work timing can find it difficult regarding the delivery time slots by e-retailers while online grocery shopping, this can be solved by asking them choosing delivery slots as per their convenience and timing, it can also be done by partnering with any local delivery services that specializes in accessibility.

Limitations of The Study

This study takes into consideration only female consumers of Indore region. Women of all other regions were excluded from the scope of this study with a view for in depth study of women of this particular region even male consumers were also not part of this study. The influence of demographical factors while online grocery shopping may vary with change in time.

Conclusion

In the present study it has been found with the help of the anova single factor test the difference between the various demographical factors and their influence on their grocery shopping online. It has been found that educational qualification and monthly household income of the consumers have positive relationship with the decision of them purchasing grocery online. More educated people tends to be more techno savvy and aware about the technological development as compared to other less educated people. Also people earning more monthly income with spend more amount on household expenses as compared to the other earning less. So this study focuses on all such demographical factors which have impact on the grocery shopping of the female consumers.

References

1. Sulaiman, A., Ng, J. and Mohezar, S. (2008) ' E-Ticketing as a new way of buying tickets: Malaysian perceptions', Journal of Social Science, vol. 17, no. 2, pp. 149-157.

2.Kim, E.Y. and Kim, Y.K. (2004) 'Predicting online purchase intention for clothing products', European Journal of Marketing, vol. 38, no. 7, pp. 883–897.

3.Armstrong, G. and Kotler, P. (2003) Marketing: An Introduction, Pearson Education International. Bakos, Y.J. (1997) 'Reducing Buyer Search Costs: Implications for Electronic Marketplaces', Management Science, vol. 43, no. 12, p. 1676–1692.

4. Brown, S.A. and Venkatesh, V. (2005) 'Model of adoption of technology in household: A baseline model test and extension incorporating household life cycle', MIS Quarterly, vol. 29, no. 3, pp. 399–426.

5. Hashim, A., Ghani, E.K. and Said, J. (2009) 'Does Consumers' Demographic Profile Influence Online Shopping?: An Examination Using Fishbein's Theory', Canadian Social Science, vol. 5, no. 6, pp. 19-31.

6. Lohse, G.L. and Spiller, P. (2000) 'Internet retail store design: how the user interface influences traffic and sales', Journal of

Computer Mediated Communication, vol. 5, no. 2, pp. 219-234.

7. Monsuwé, T.P., Dellaert, B.G.C. and de Ruyter, K. (2004) 'What drives consumer to shop online? A literature review', International Journal of Service Industry Management, vol. 15, no. 1, pp. 102-121.

CHAPTER XII

"Enhancing Aerospace Engineering through Artificial Intelligence: Applications in Design Optimization, Predictive Maintenance, and Autonomous Flight S

Mr. Aaradhya Sharma
Pursuing B. Tech. in Aero Space, VIT, Bhopal
Dr. Danish Khan
Assistant Professor, St. Paul Institute of Professional Studies, Indore

Abstract

This research paper explores the transformative role of Artificial Intelligence (AI) in aerospace engineering, focusing on three key areas: design optimization, predictive maintenance, and autonomous flight systems. The study investigates how AI algorithms can streamline the design process, improve the efficiency and safety of aircraft, and reduce operational costs. Additionally, the paper examines the application of AI in predictive maintenance, where machine learning models can predict potential failures, thus minimizing downtime and enhancing the longevity of aerospace components. Furthermore, the research delves into the development of autonomous flight systems, highlighting how AI can enable unmanned aerial vehicles (UAVs) and drones to operate safely and efficiently in various environments. The goal is to provide a comprehensive overview of how AI is reshaping the aerospace industry, paving the way for smarter, safer, and more sustainable aviation solutions.

Introduction

The aerospace industry stands at the forefront of technological advancement, driven by the need for increased efficiency, safety, and innovation. As aerospace engineering continues to evolve, the integration of Artificial Intelligence (AI) has emerged as a transformative force, offering new opportunities to enhance various aspects of the field. AI, with its capabilities in machine learning, data analysis, and automation, holds the potential to revolutionize aerospace engineering by optimizing design processes, improving maintenance practices, and enabling autonomous flight systems.

In aerospace design, AI techniques are being employed to optimize aerodynamic shapes, reduce material usage, and accelerate the design process. Predictive maintenance powered by AI is transforming how aircraft components are monitored and maintained, allowing for proactive management that minimizes downtime and extends the lifespan of critical parts. Autonomous flight systems, driven by AI, are paving the way for innovations in unmanned aerial vehicles (UAVs) and drones, offering advancements in navigation, obstacle avoidance, and operational efficiency.

This research paper aims to explore the impact of AI on aerospace engineering by focusing on three primary areas: design optimization, predictive maintenance, and autonomous flight systems. By examining current applications, challenges, and future trends, the paper seeks to provide a comprehensive overview of how AI is reshaping the aerospace industry, highlighting its potential benefits and addressing key concerns.

Literature Review

1. AI in Design Optimization

The integration of AI in aerospace design optimization has garnered significant attention in recent years. AI techniques, such as genetic algorithms, neural networks, and reinforcement learning, are increasingly utilized to enhance the efficiency of design processes. According to Ghosh et al. (2021), AI-driven optimization methods enable the exploration of complex design spaces, leading to innovations in aerodynamic efficiency and structural performance. For instance, machine learning algorithms can predict optimal design parameters, reduce the need for iterative testing, and accelerate time-to-market for new aerospace components.

A study by Chen et al. (2019) highlights the use of AI in optimizing wing designs for aircraft. The researchers employed neural networks to predict aerodynamic performance and identify design improvements, resulting in more efficient and fuel-effective wing structures. These advancements illustrate the potential of AI to not only enhance traditional design methodologies but also to unlock new possibilities in aerospace engineering.

2. Predictive Maintenance Using AI

Predictive maintenance is a critical area where AI is making a substantial impact. Traditional maintenance practices often rely on scheduled inspections and reactive repairs, which can be costly and inefficient. AI technologies, such as predictive analytics and anomaly detection, offer a proactive approach to maintenance by forecasting potential failures before they occur. According to a review by Zhang et al. (2020), AI models can analyze historical data, sensor readings, and operational conditions to predict component failures, optimize maintenance schedules, and reduce operational disruptions.

The implementation of AI in predictive maintenance is exemplified by Boeing's use of machine learning to monitor aircraft systems. The company has developed algorithms that analyze real-time data from various sensors to predict potential malfunctions and recommend timely interventions. This approach not only enhances safety but also contributes to cost savings and operational efficiency.

3. Autonomous Flight Systems

Autonomous flight systems represent a significant advancement in aerospace engineering, driven by AI technologies. UAVs and drones, powered by AI algorithms, are capable of performing complex flight operations with minimal human intervention. AI enables these systems to navigate, avoid obstacles, and adapt to dynamic environments. Research by Wang et al. (2021) demonstrates the use of deep learning for autonomous navigation in drones, where AI models process real-time imagery to identify obstacles and make flight decisions.

Additionally, AI-powered autonomous systems are being explored for space exploration and satellite management. According to a study by Kwon et al. (2022), AI is used to control and optimize satellite operations, such as orbit adjustments and data collection. This capability is crucial for managing large fleets of satellites and ensuring the success of space missions.

4. Challenges and Future Trends

Despite the promising advancements, the integration of AI in aerospace engineering faces several challenges. Technical issues, such as data quality, algorithmic transparency, and system integration, must be addressed to fully realize the potential of AI. A review by Smith et al. (2023) highlights the importance of developing robust AI systems that can operate reliably in the highly regulated and safety-critical aerospace environment.

Looking ahead, the future of AI in aerospace engineering is expected to be shaped by continued advancements in AI technologies, including quantum computing and edge AI. These innovations will likely drive further improvements in design optimization, maintenance practices, and autonomous systems, paving the way for more advanced and efficient aerospace solutions.

Objectives
1. To Assess the Impact of AI on Aerospace Design Optimization
2. To Evaluate the Role of AI in Predictive Maintenance for Aerospace Systems
3. To Explore the Development and Implementation of Autonomous Flight Systems in Aerospace Engineering

Findings and Discussion

1. Impact of AI on Aerospace Design Optimization

Findings:

- **Design Efficiency:** AI techniques, such as generative design and optimization algorithms, have significantly enhanced the efficiency of aerospace design processes. For instance, machine learning algorithms can analyze vast datasets to identify design patterns that improve aerodynamic performance. This results in more efficient designs that can reduce fuel consumption and increase overall performance.
- **Material Utilization:** AI has enabled the optimization of material usage in aerospace components. Through advanced simulations and predictive models, AI can determine the optimal materials and structures that balance strength, weight, and cost. This contributes to lighter and more efficient aircraft

designs.

- **Accelerated Design Cycles:** AI tools, including optimization algorithms and simulation software, have reduced the time required for aerospace design. By automating complex calculations and simulations, AI accelerates the design process, leading to faster prototyping and deployment of new aerospace technologies.

Discussion:

AI-driven design optimization has transformed aerospace engineering by enabling more efficient and effective design processes. The integration of AI in design allows engineers to explore a wider range of design alternatives and evaluate their performance in a fraction of the time compared to traditional methods. However, challenges remain in integrating AI tools with existing design workflows and ensuring that AI-generated designs meet all safety and regulatory standards.

2. Role of AI in Predictive Maintenance for Aerospace Systems

Findings:
- **Enhanced Reliability:** Predictive maintenance, powered by AI, has improved the reliability of aerospace systems by using machine learning models to predict component failures before they occur. This proactive approach minimizes unexpected breakdowns and enhances overall system reliability.
- **Cost Savings:** Implementing AI-driven predictive maintenance can result in significant cost savings by reducing the need for scheduled maintenance and preventing costly repairs. AI systems analyze sensor data and historical maintenance records to predict failures, enabling targeted maintenance activities that optimize resource utilization.
- **Challenges:** Despite its benefits, AI-driven predictive maintenance faces challenges such as the need for large volumes

of high-quality data and the complexity of integrating AI systems with existing maintenance processes. Additionally, ensuring the accuracy and reliability of AI predictions is critical to avoid false positives and negatives.

Discussion:

AI's role in predictive maintenance represents a significant advancement in aerospace engineering, enhancing the reliability and cost-effectiveness of maintenance practices. By shifting from reactive to proactive maintenance strategies, AI helps airlines and aerospace companies manage their assets more effectively. However, the successful implementation of predictive maintenance requires addressing challenges related to data quality, system integration, and the interpretability of AI predictions.

3. Development and Implementation of Autonomous Flight Systems

Findings:
- **Autonomous Navigation:** AI technologies, including computer vision and machine learning algorithms, have enabled significant advancements in autonomous flight systems. UAVs and drones equipped with AI can navigate complex environments, avoid obstacles, and perform tasks with minimal human intervention.
- **Safety and Efficiency:** AI enhances the safety and efficiency of autonomous flight systems by enabling real-time decision-making and adaptive responses to dynamic conditions. AI systems can process data from various sensors to make informed decisions, improving the reliability of autonomous flight operations.

Future Prospects: The development of autonomous flight systems is poised to revolutionize aerospace operations, including space exploration and satellite management. AI's ability to handle complex tasks and adapt to changing environments positions it as a key enabler of future aerospace innovations.

Discussion:

The integration of AI into autonomous flight systems has expanded the capabilities and applications of UAVs and drones, paving the way for new aerospace technologies and missions. While the benefits of autonomous flight are evident, challenges related to safety, regulatory compliance, and public acceptance must be addressed. Continued research and development in AI will be essential to overcome these challenges and fully realize the potential of autonomous flight systems.

Recommendations

Integration of AI in Design Processes:

Adopt Advanced AI Tools: Aerospace companies should integrate state-of-the-art AI tools and algorithms into their design processes. This includes using generative design software and optimization algorithms to enhance design efficiency and material utilization.

Training and Skill Development: Invest in training programs for engineers and designers to effectively utilize AI tools. Developing skills in AI-driven design techniques will ensure that teams can fully leverage these technologies.

Enhancing Predictive Maintenance:

Implement AI-Based Predictive Maintenance Systems: Aerospace organizations should implement AI-powered predictive maintenance systems to improve reliability and reduce maintenance costs. This includes deploying sensors and data analytics platforms that can provide real-time insights into equipment health.

Data Quality and Integration: Focus on improving data quality and ensuring seamless integration of AI systems with existing maintenance workflows. High-quality, accurate data is crucial for the effectiveness of predictive maintenance algorithms.

Advancing Autonomous Flight Technologies:

Invest in Research and Development: Continue to invest in R&D for autonomous flight systems to advance capabilities and address safety concerns. This includes developing robust AI algorithms for navigation, obstacle avoidance, and decision-making in complex environments.

Regulatory and Safety Standards: Collaborate with regulatory bodies to establish safety standards and regulations for autonomous flight systems. Ensuring compliance with these standards will facilitate the safe and responsible deployment of autonomous technologies.

Ethical and Responsible AI Use:

Develop Ethical Guidelines: Establish ethical guidelines for the use of AI in aerospace engineering, addressing concerns related to data privacy, transparency, and accountability. These guidelines will help ensure that AI applications align with ethical standards and societal expectations.

Regular Audits and Assessments: Conduct regular audits and assessments of AI systems to evaluate their performance, identify potential biases, and ensure compliance with ethical guidelines. Continuous monitoring will help mitigate risks and enhance the overall reliability of AI applications.

Promote Collaboration and Knowledge Sharing:

Foster Industry Collaboration: Encourage collaboration between aerospace companies, AI researchers, and technology providers to share knowledge and best practices. Joint efforts can accelerate the development and deployment of innovative AI solutions.

Participate in Industry Forums: Engage in industry forums and conferences to stay updated on the latest advancements in AI and aerospace engineering. Participation in these events will facilitate knowledge exchange and foster partnerships.

Conclusion

The integration of Artificial Intelligence into aerospace engineering holds transformative potential, particularly in the areas of design optimization, predictive maintenance, and autonomous flight systems. AI technologies have demonstrated the ability to enhance design efficiency, improve maintenance practices, and advance autonomous capabilities, thereby contributing to the progress of the aerospace industry.

However, the successful implementation of AI in aerospace engineering requires addressing several challenges, including ensuring data quality, integrating AI systems with existing processes, and adhering to safety and ethical standards. By adopting advanced AI tools, investing in training, and developing robust ethical guidelines, aerospace organizations can maximize the benefits of AI while mitigating associated risks.

The future of aerospace engineering will likely be shaped by continued advancements in AI technology, driving innovation and efficiency across various applications. Ongoing research, collaboration, and proactive measures will be essential to harness the full potential of AI and ensure its responsible and effective use in the aerospace industry.

Limited Access to Data: The research may be constrained by limited access to comprehensive and high-quality data on AI applications in aerospace engineering. The effectiveness of AI systems is heavily dependent on the quality of data, and insufficient data can hinder accurate analysis and evaluation.

Data Privacy Concerns: The use of sensitive or proprietary data from aerospace companies may raise privacy and confidentiality issues, restricting the depth of analysis and the scope of findings.

Limitations of the ResearchData Availability and Quality:

Technological Constraints:
- **Rapidly Evolving Technology:** The field of AI in aerospace is rapidly evolving, which means that findings may quickly become outdated as new technologies and methodologies emerge. The pace of technological advancement can outstrip the ability to conduct comprehensive and up-to-date research.
- **Integration Challenges:** Practical integration of AI systems into existing aerospace workflows may face technical challenges and resistance from established practices. These challenges can affect the implementation and effectiveness of AI solutions.

Ethical and Regulatory Uncertainties:
- **Lack of Strandardized Guidelines:** There is a lack of standardized ethical guidelines and regulatory frameworks for AI applications in aerospace engineering. The absence of established standards can lead to variability in practices and

difficulties in ensuring compliance

- **Unpredictable Implications:** The long-term ethical and societal implications of deploying AI in aerospace are still uncertain. Predicting and addressing these implications can be challenging and may require ongoing evaluation and adaptation.

Limited Scope of Case Studies:

- **Small Sample Size:** The research may rely on a limited number of case studies or pilot projects, which may not be representative of the broader industry. This limitation can affect the generalizability of the findings and recommendations.

Interdisciplinary Complexity:

- **Complex Interactions:** The intersection of AI and aerospace engineering involves complex interactions between multiple disciplines, including engineering, computer science, and ethics. The complexity of these interactions may limit the ability to fully explore and address all relevant aspects.

Future Scope

Expansion of Data Sources:

- **Enhanced Data Collection:** Future research should focus on expanding data sources and improving data collection methods to obtain more comprehensive and high-quality data on AI applications in aerospace. Collaborations with industry partners and data-sharing initiatives could facilitate this.

Longitudinal Studies:

- **Ongoing Monitoring:** Conducting longitudinal studies to track the long-term impacts of AI technologies in aerospace engineering will provide valuable insights into their effectiveness, challenges, and evolving trends over time.

Development of Standardized Guidelines:

- **Ethical Frameworks and Regulations:** Future research should contribute to the development of standardized ethical frameworks and regulatory guidelines for AI applications in aerospace. Establishing clear standards will help ensure responsible and effective use of AI technologies.

Exploration of Emerging Technologies:

- **New AI Techniques:** Investigate emerging AI technologies and methodologies, such as advanced machine learning algorithms and quantum computing, to explore their potential applications and benefits in aerospace engineering.

Broader Industry Impact:

- **Industry-Wide Surveys:** Conduct surveys and studies across a broader range of aerospace organizations to assess the widespread impact of AI technologies. This will help identify common challenges and best practices applicable to the industry as a whole.

Interdisciplinary Collaboration:

- **Cross-Disciplinary Research:** Encourage interdisciplinary research that integrates insights from AI, aerospace engineering, ethics, and regulatory studies. Collaborative efforts between experts in these fields will provide a more holistic understanding of AI's role and implications in aerospace.

Ethical and Societal Impact Studies:

- **In-Depth Ethical Analysis:** Future research should include in-depth studies of the ethical and societal impacts of AI in aerospace, focusing on issues such as privacy, bias, and job displacement. This will help address potential concerns and develop strategies for mitigating negative effects.

By addressing these limitations and exploring the outlined future directions, researchers and industry stakeholders can advance the integration of AI in aerospace engineering and contribute to the development of innovative, ethical, and effective solutions.

References

1.Izzo, Dario, Marcus Märtens, and Binfeng Pan. "A survey on artificial intelligence trends in spacecraft guidance dynamics and control." Astrodynamics 2019, 3: 287-299.

2.Vasile, M., Minisci, E., Locatelli, M. Analysis of some global optimization algorithms for space trajectory design. Journal of Spacecraft and Rockets, 2010, 47(2): 334–344.

3.Englander, J. A., Conway, B. A., Williams, T. Automated mission planning via evolutionary algorithms. Journal of Guidance, Control, and Dynamics, 2012, 35(6): 1878–1887.

4.Vasile, M., Ricciardi, L. A direct memetic approach to the solution of multi-objective optimal control problems. Proceedings of 2016 IEEE Symposium Series on Computational Intelligence, 2016, 1–8.

5.Emami, Seyyed Ali, Paolo Castaldi, and Afshin Banazadeh. "Neural network-based flight control systems: Present and future." Annual Reviews in Control, 2022, 53: 97-137.

6. Lary, David John. "Artificial intelligence in geoscience and remote sensing." Geoscience and Remote Sensing New Achievements. IntechOpen, 2010, 1-9.

7.Wu Yingnian, Xie Jianwen, Lu Yang, et al. Sparse and Deep Generalizations of the FRAME Model. Annals of Mathematical Sciences and Applications, 2018, 3(1):1-9

8.Wang, Lizhe, et al. "Knowledge discovery from remote sensing images: A review." International journal of remote sensing, 2012, 33.13: 4057-4082.

9.Wiley Interdisciplinary Reviews: Data Mining and Knowledge Discovery 2020, 10.5: e1371.

10.Beltrán-González, Carlos, Matteo Bustreo, and Alessio Del Bue. "External and internal quality inspection of aerospace components." 2020 IEEE 7th international workshop on metrology for aerospace, 1-12.

11.Xiao, Yuling, and Haoran Zhang. "Research on surface crack detection technology based on digital image processing." Journal of Physics: Conference Series. 2020, 1550. 3.

12.Shokirov, Rakhimjon, et al. "Prospects of the development of unmanned aerial vehicles (UAVs)." Technical science and innovation, 2020.3: 4-8.

13.Q. Zhang, M. Mozaffari, W. Saad, M. Bennis and M. Debbah, "Machine learning for predictive on-demand deployment of UAVs for wireless communications", Proc. IEEE Global Commun. Conf., 2018, 1-9.

14. Bozcan and E. Kayacan, UAV-AdNet: Unsupervised anomaly detection using deep neural networks for aerial surveillance, 2020, 1-13.

15.C. Titouna, F. Nait-Abdesselam and H. Moungla, "An online anomaly detection approach for unmanned aerial vehicles", Proc. Int. Wireless Commun. Mobile Comput. 2019. 469-474

16.EarthRisk Technologies, 2013: TempRisk Apollo White Paper. Available at http://www.earthrisktech.com/resources/ reports/white_papers/TempRiskApollo_WhitePaper _Oct2013.pdf. Accessed on 16 August 2019.

CHAPTER XIII

"How AI is changing the Face of Commerce"

Ms. Ishita Jain
(Research Scholar)
Dr. Payal Jain
(Assistant Professor-Graduate School of Business, Indore)

Abstract

This paper investigates the profound impact of Artificial Intelligence (AI) on the commercial landscape, focusing on its diverse applications, advantages, and challenges. Through an extensive review of existing literature, the study reveals AI's ability to enhance customer experiences, streamline operations, and foster business growth. AI has proven especially impactful in areas such as personalization, where it tailors customer interactions, and supply chain management, where it optimizes logistics and inventory management. Additionally, predictive analytics powered by AI are enabling businesses to anticipate market trends, improving decision-making and efficiency. However, the integration of AI also presents challenges, including data privacy concerns and the need for skilled labor. Despite these challenges, AI's benefits offer substantial opportunities for businesses to gain competitive advantages in the market.

Introduction:

The emergence of Artificial Intelligence (AI) has marked the beginning of a new era in commerce, defined by unparalleled levels of efficiency, productivity, and innovation. AI's ability to analyze vast amounts of data, recognize patterns, and make informed decisions has revolutionized business operations, customer engagement, and market dynamics. In particular, AI enables real-time decision-making, allowing businesses to adapt quickly to changes in consumer behavior and market conditions. The shift toward AI-powered technologies has also facilitated the rise of automation in various sectors, reducing human error and operational costs. Furthermore, AI's potential to enhance customer experience through personalized interactions has proven crucial in gaining customer loyalty and satisfaction. As AI continues to evolve, it is expected to play an even more prominent role in shaping the future of commerce and influencing the strategies of businesses across industries.

Background:

AI's role in commerce dates back to the 1990s, when early adopters implemented rule-based systems for decision-making. These early applications were primarily focused on automating routine tasks and optimizing basic business processes. Over time, however, AI technologies evolved to include machine learning, which allowed systems to improve their performance through data analysis. The rapid development of natural language processing and computer vision in the last decade has significantly expanded AI's capabilities, enabling it to process and understand complex data, such as unstructured text and images. These advancements have opened the door to more sophisticated applications in commerce, from chatbots offering personalized customer service to AI-driven supply chain management systems. As AI technologies become increasingly integrated into business operations, their potential to drive innovation and competitive advantage continues to grow, making AI an essential tool for modern commerce.

Objective of Study:

To examine the impact of Artificial Intelligence (AI) on commerce, focusing on:
1. Identifying AI-driven innovations in commerce.
2. Analyzing the benefits and challenges of AI adoption.

Literature Review:

Dr. S. Shanmugapriya, S. Pavithra (2024) The integration of Artificial Intelligence (AI) and Machine Learning (ML) into the e-commerce industry has revolutionized online shopping by enhancing personalization and improving customer experiences. Research indicates that AI-driven marketing strategies, powered by customer data, lead to better-targeted campaigns and product recommendations. AI also plays a crucial role in customer retention through automation and intelligent chatbots, significantly enhancing customer satisfaction and loyalty. Additionally, AI's automation capabilities allow businesses to scale efficiently while optimizing costs and improving overall operational performance.

Amina Badreddine (2024) Artificial intelligence (AI) plays a crucial role in E-commerce by enhancing customer experience and improving operational efficiency. It powers chatbots and virtual assistants that provide 24/7 support, offers personalized product recommendations based on customer behavior, and enables AI-driven personalization to enhance services. Additionally, AI helps track product demand and inventory levels, ensuring efficient stock management. With its significant impact, businesses are heavily investing in AI to remain competitive and meet the growing demands of consumers.

Alejandro Valencia-Arias, Hernán Uribe-Bedoya (2024) this bibliometric study explores the growing intersection of recommendation systems and AI in E-commerce, revealing a

97.16% increase in research output. Analyzing 91 of 120 documents, the study identifies key contributors like Paraschakis and Nilsson, as well as influential publications such as Electronic Commerce Research. China leads in citations, with India contributing significantly to the field. Research has notably increased in 2021 and 2022, with a shift toward sentiment analysis and convolutional neural networks. Emerging keywords like content-based image retrieval and knowledge graphs suggest promising areas for future exploration in AI-driven E-commerce.

Manpreet Singh (2023) AI has revolutionized e-commerce by enabling voice commerce through voice assistants, allowing customers to make hands-free purchases. This simplifies the buying process and enhances the shopping experience. AI also provides personalized recommendations, efficient customer service, and accurate demand forecasting, and improved search capabilities. Additionally, it optimizes pricing, enhances security, and streamlines supply chain operations. By adopting AI technologies, e-commerce businesses can remain competitive, boost customer satisfaction, and foster growth in the dynamic digital marketplace.

Ms J.Prabha, Dr. M G R (2021) the analysis reveals varying user experiences with e-commerce, highlighting that 45.8% of respondents have used e-commerce for less than a year, with 37.5% using it for 1 to 5 years. A majority (50%) are involved in banking, followed by 30.3% in other domains, and 12.7% in travel and tourism. In terms of satisfaction, 41.7% of respondents rated their experience as very good, indicating that AI-driven enhancements have contributed significantly to improving user experiences on e-commerce platforms. Intelligent marketers are increasingly leveraging AI for AI-enhanced PPC advertising, creating highly personalized website experiences, improving conversion rate optimization (CRO), and utilizing AI-powered content creation and content-creation chatbots to further enhance user engagement and satisfaction.

Neha Soni, Enakshi Khular Sharma (2020) the rise of AI start-ups demonstrates significant global market impact, with rapid growth in sectors like business intelligence, healthcare, cybersecurity, and marketing. AI's benefits, including increased productivity and cost efficiency, are evident. However, regional disparities in AI adoption create an "AI divide," exacerbating inequalities. Challenges such as algorithm reliability, trust, ethics, and talent shortages also hinder AI's widespread commercial use and adoption.

Outcome of Literature Review:

The integration of Artificial Intelligence (AI) and Machine Learning (ML) in the e-commerce industry has significantly transformed online shopping, creating enhanced personalization, improved customer experiences, and streamlined operations. The literature review highlights key findings from several studies on the growing role of AI in e-commerce.

Personalization and Customer Experience: AI has become a cornerstone for personalizing the online shopping experience. According to Dr. S. Shanmugapriya and S. Pavithra (2024), AI-driven marketing strategies leverage customer data to create targeted campaigns and personalized product recommendations, improving customer satisfaction. Additionally, AI-powered chatbots and virtual assistants enable 24/7 support, driving customer retention and loyalty (Amina Badreddine, 2024).

Automation and Operational Efficiency: AI's ability to automate customer service and various operational processes is crucial for business scalability and cost optimization. The use of intelligent chatbots not only boosts customer service but also aids in inventory management and demand forecasting (Amina Badreddine, 2024). This reduces operational inefficiencies and enhances the overall business performance.

Voice Commerce and Simplified Purchasing: As highlighted by Manpreet Singh (2023), AI has also introduced voice commerce, allowing customers to make purchases via voice commands. This hands-free shopping experience simplifies the buying process and adds a new layer of convenience for users.

Increasing Research and Development in AI: The bibliometric study by Alejandro Valencia-Arias and Hernán Uribe-Bedoya (2024) highlights a 97.16% increase in research output regarding AI and recommendation systems in e-commerce. The study notes a shift toward technologies like sentiment analysis and convolutional neural networks, indicating areas of continued growth and exploration.

Regional Disparities and the "AI Divide": A notable challenge identified by Neha Soni and Enakshi Khular Sharma (2020) is the regional disparity in AI adoption, leading to an "AI divide." This divide could exacerbate social and economic inequalities, limiting access to AI's benefits in certain regions. Furthermore, challenges like algorithm reliability, trust issues, and talent shortages remain significant barriers to the widespread commercial use of AI.

AI's Role in Marketing and Advertising: Ms. J. Prabha and Dr. M. G R (2021) emphasize that AI-enhanced pay-per-click (PPC) advertising and website personalization have improved conversion rates and customer engagement. AI's ability to create tailored experiences for users enhances marketing effectiveness, contributing to better conversion and retention rates.

In conclusion, AI's integration into e-commerce has not only revolutionized customer experience but also improved operational efficiency. The continuous rise in research and development signals a strong future for AI in e-commerce, although challenges like the AI divide and ethical concerns remain key areas for attention. To stay competitive, businesses must leverage AI for personalized services, operational optimization, and enhanced customer engagement.

Challenges

Despite the transformative potential of AI in e-commerce, several challenges remain that can hinder its full integration and effectiveness. These include issues related to data quality and integration, AI bias and ethics, talent acquisition and training, regulatory frameworks, and cyber security concerns.

Data Quality and Integration: AI relies heavily on data to function effectively. However, poor-quality data, such as incomplete, outdated, or inconsistent data, can lead to inaccurate insights and suboptimal decision-making. In e-commerce, integrating data from various sources (e.g., customer behavior, sales transactions, and inventory) can be complex and time-consuming. Ensuring data quality and seamless integration across platforms is essential for AI algorithms to provide accurate and reliable results.

AI Bias and Ethics: AI systems can inherit biases from the data they are trained on. This is especially concerning in e-commerce, where biased algorithms can lead to unfair practices, such as discrimination in product recommendations or pricing. Addressing AI bias involves improving the diversity and representativeness of training data, as well as implementing ethical guidelines to ensure fairness, transparency, and accountability in AI-driven decisions.

Talent Acquisition and Training: The rapid advancement of AI requires skilled professionals who can develop, implement, and maintain AI systems. However, there is a significant shortage of AI talent, particularly in specialized areas such as machine learning, data science, and AI ethics. E-commerce companies face challenges in attracting and retaining skilled professionals, leading to an increased demand for training and upskilling existing employees to bridge this talent gap.

Regulatory Frameworks: The regulatory landscape for AI in e-commerce is still evolving. As AI technologies rapidly advance, regulators are striving to keep up with ensuring privacy, data protection, and consumer rights. E-commerce businesses must navigate varying regulations across regions, which can complicate AI implementation and compliance, particularly regarding consumer data and cross-border transactions.

Cyber security Concerns: The use of AI in e-commerce introduces new cyber security risks. AI systems can be vulnerable to attacks, such as adversarial machine learning, where malicious actors manipulate the system's learning process. Additionally, as AI increasingly handles sensitive consumer data, ensuring robust cyber security measures to prevent data breaches and unauthorized access becomes a critical concern for e-commerce businesses.

Addressing these challenges is crucial to ensure AI's responsible, secure, and effective application in e-commerce.

Conclusion:

In conclusion, the integration of AI and ML into the e-commerce sector has profoundly transformed the industry, driving enhanced personalization, improved customer experiences, and operational efficiencies. AI-driven marketing strategies, personalized product recommendations, intelligent chatbots, and voice commerce have significantly impacted customer satisfaction, retention, and business scalability. The rising investment in AI research and development underscores its growing importance in e-commerce, with promising advancements in sentiment analysis, convolutional neural networks, and recommendation systems.

However, the widespread adoption of AI in e-commerce faces

several challenges. Data quality and integration remain key concerns, as poor or fragmented data can compromise AI's effectiveness. Moreover, issues of AI bias and ethics, along with the need for more skilled talent, must be addressed to ensure fairness, transparency, and the responsible use of AI technologies. The evolving regulatory frameworks and the growing need for robust cybersecurity measures further complicate the landscape, as businesses must navigate complex rules and safeguard consumer data.

While AI holds tremendous potential to drive innovation and growth in e-commerce, overcoming these challenges is essential for unlocking its full capabilities. Businesses must invest in data quality, ethical AI practices, talent development, regulatory compliance, and cybersecurity to maintain a competitive edge and foster trust in their AI-powered solutions. The future of e-commerce hinges on the successful integration of AI, addressing both the opportunities and challenges it presents to create a more personalized, efficient, and secure shopping experience for consumers.

References:

1.https://hal.science/hal-04379642v1/document
2.https://jrps.shodhsagar.com/index.php/j/article/view/409/406
3.https://www.researchgate.net/publication/
379566725_ARTIFICIAL_INTELLIGENCE_AND_E-COMMERCE
4.https://ijcrt.org/papers/IJCRTG020005.pdf
5.https://www.sciencedirect.com/science/article/pii/
S1877050920307389
6.Chen, Y., et al. (2020). AI-powered cybersecurity for commerce: A systematic review. Journal of Electronic Commerce Research, 20(1), 1-18.
7.Huang, Y., et al. (2019). AI-powered customer service: A study on chatbots and virtual assistants. Journal of Service Research, 22(3), 279-294.

www.ingramcontent.com/pod-product-compliance
Lightning Source LLC
Chambersburg PA
CBHW031626170726
47990CB00017B/384